CW00544929

Endangered Ecosystems

Rights of Nature Protection for the Benefit of Both Ecosystems and Individual Species

Jay Cooper Beeks, Ph.D. (Arizona State University); Alexander Ziko (Franklin Pierce University); Nicole Cox (Arizona State University) and Sukhmani Singh (Arizona State University)

Published by The Green Economics Institute

2021

The Green Economics Institute

Endangered Ecosystems:
Rights of Nature Protection for the Benefit of Both Ecosystems and Individual Species

Published by The Green Economics Institute
www.greeneconomicsinstitute.org.uk

Registered Office: 6 Strachey Close, Tidmarsh, Reading RG8 8EP

greeneconomicsinstitute@yahoo.com
and
info@geibooks.org.uk

www.geibooks.org.uk

Dr Jay Beeks, Alexander Ziko, Nicole Cox and Sukhmani Singh

Printed on FSC approved stock by Marston Book Services Ltd and PrintForce.

A catalogue record for this book is available from the British Library

2

This edited volume has been assembled solely for the use of Readers of *Endangered Ecosystems: Rights of Nature Protection for the Benefit of Both Ecosystems and Individual Species* is lodged with the British Library and for publication by the Green Economics Institute. Copyright for the Volume rests with the Green Economics Institute. Copyright for each individual chapter rests jointly with the respective author(s) photographer, editor and The Green Economics Institute.

Written permission must be sought in all cases from the relevant author(s) of papers, chapters, herein and photographs and The Green Economics Institute to reproduce by any means, circulate or distribute the contents or any part of the contents of this book. Some chapters are subject also to other additional copyrights and so written permission must be sought from us at greeneconomicsinstitute@yahoo.com or the originating publishers, before any copying can take place. If any words, papers, chapters, ideas, diagrams, or photos or other material are used as reference, in other subsequent work, full citation must be given and such rights are enforced by us and other publishers we work with, who may also have a claim on them.

The texts contained within this book remain in the form submitted by the individual authors with minor edits for practical reasons, including removal of certain graphs, tables and wording where necessary. The Green Economics Institute does not accept responsibility for any textual or factual inaccuracies within this book and whilst they represent the views of the author, they may not necessarily represent the views of the Institute.

Citation: This book should be cited as "Beeks J., Ziko A., Cox N., & *Singh S,. Editors. (2020). 'Endangered Ecosystems: Rights of Nature Protection for the Benefit of Both Ecosystems and Individual Species'* The Green Economics Institute, Reading. UK."

Disclaimer: Views expressed are not necessarily the views of the Green Economics Institute and the Editors reserve the right to edit all chapters. *Endangered Ecosystems: Rights of Nature for the Benefit of Both Ecosystems and Individual Species* is a publication of The Green Economics Institute.

Contents

About The Green Economics Institute

The Green Economics Institute has been working to create and establish a discipline or school of Economics called "Green Economics", which aims to change cultural norms and seeks to reform mainstream economics itself into a well-defined goals-based discipline which provides practical answers to existing and future problems by incorporating all relevant aspects, knowledge and complex interactions into a truly holistic understanding of the relevant issues.

Uncontrolled Growth and the high mass consumption which accompanies it over the last 40 years have created an over exhaustion of the planet's resources and an unhealthy, unsustainable and unequal society in which 99% of people are economically disempowered. The world's economy, instead of concentrating on well-being for all people, has turned into a machine to please approximately 1% of the global population and who continue to act in their own self interest. This economic model has only served to create social unrest and geo-political instability.

The Green Economics Institute exists to educate the public about the very real choices available to them and how they can indeed choose to do things differently. It uses complexity, holistic thinking, pluralism and interdisciplinary working in order to widen the scope of economics, adding the science from the green aspects, and the social ideas from economics discourses. This new approach aims to avoid the partial explanations and solutions of the past as well as the often biased perspectives of powerful elites.

The Institute seeks to provide all people, non-human species, the planet and earth systems with a decent level of well-being based on practical and theoretical approaches targeting both methodology and knowledge and based on a comprehensive reform of the current economic mainstream. It can, for example, comfortably incorporate glacial issues, climate change and volcanic, seismic and earth sciences into its explanations and thus in this, and many other ways, it is far more complete and reflects reality much more closely than its predecessors on which it builds.

The Green Economics Institute argues for economic development based on economic access and decision making for all, including respect for cultural diversity and normative freedom. It does this by bringing together all the interested parties, who want to help in developing this progressive discipline, by inviting them to events, and

7

conferences and by means of such activities as writing books and publications and using its research, campaigns, and lecturing all over the world.

The Green Economics Institute created the world's first green academic journal *International Journal of Green Economics* with publishers Inderscience. The journal is gender balanced and includes a diverse range of authors from across the globe. It is also multi and interdisciplinary and aims to encourage economic change by positioning Green Economics at the centre of the Economics disciplines.

Green Economic theories, policies, tools, instruments and metrics are developed to facilitate a change to the current economic models for the benefit of the widest number of people and for the planet as a whole. The journal focuses particularly on resource management, meeting peoples' needs and the impact and effects of international trends and how to increase social justice.

In June 2019, our official United Nations Delegation, side event and exhibition stand at UNFCC HQ pressed for faster uptake of climate solutions and ambition and aimed to build on the support we received for our ideas in Katowice at COP24 and also COP23 in Bonn. Our official United Nations Delegation participated in the United Nations Climate Conference in December

2019 at Madrid COP25. Our Green Charter for the Cities event with partners, the Green European Foundation, was held in Oxford in August 2019.

The Green Economics Institute carries out cutting edge research and out of the box thinking in a variety of ways. Our books provide the resources built from our research projects. Our books are unique, diverse, and inclusive. We have a series of more than 100 books and academic proceedings from the conferences we have run over the last 15 years.

The Green Economics Institute focuses on the practical consequences of educational policy decisions and alternatives. Our team develops an innovative relationship between educational policy and educational practice that sheds new lights on important debates and controversies within trans-disciplinary and interdisciplinary fields of research. In line with this perspective, new training courses and the Green Economics Institute Summer School are part of the education agenda. In addition to training students all around the world, we train and advise ministries, treasuries, ambassadors and prime ministers. The Green Economics Institute´s expertise in Green economics, social and environmental justice and reform of economics of 25 years involves lecturing, tutorials and training at the highest levels of universities, government and many other institutions. The Green Economics Institute is pleased to develop its series of Master Classes around the world linking its unique network of people from all walks of life, all united in aiming to raise the ambition to reform economics, stop runaway climate change and reverse it and stop the 6th ever mass extinction of species.

This network prides itself on its inclusion, diversity, access for everyone. It bases its work on the extensive Green Economics body of literature, and innovative theories, policy making and writings to come out of the Institute over the last 18 years.

The Green Economics Institute was founded to protect Eco Systems and to educate the public about the 6th ever Mass Extinction on earth. This book is published on a day when a report came out from The World Wildlife Fund (WWF) Living Planet Report 2020, showing an average 68% decline in animal population sizes tracked over 46 years (1970-2016) just one or two generations!

It is vitally important that we all understand how everything is linked and destroying one part of an ecosystem upsets and destroys the rest of it. This book explains the dynamics of how this happens and how the world is constructed and as such is a very useful addition to the literature and we are delighted to welcome it into our collection of lovely books.

About the Authors

Jay Cooper Beeks, Ph.D. (Arizona State University)

Dr. Beeks' focus now is as a full-time instructor at Arizona State University (ASU) for the School of Sustainability (SOS) for undergraduate studies in the Julie Ann Wrigley Global Institute of Sustainability. His past teaching experience includes multiple courses at Marylhurst University for the Sustainable MBA program, the University of Denver for the Masters in Recreational Management program, Franklin Pierce University for the Energy and Sustainability M.S. program, at Saint Francis University for the Sustainability MBA program and at ASU for the Masters in

Sustainability Leadership program. A few of these courses include sustainable leadership, sustainable transportation, renewable energy, integrated environmental systems, basic energy science, introduction to sustainability, global energy, business modeling and decision making, industrial hygiene, equity - justice and sustainability, site evaluation and remediation, impacts of recreational use and principles of sustainability.

Alexander Ziko (Franklin Pierce University)

Alexander Ziko is a data analyst for Rapid Insight, a data and predictive modeling software company located in New Hampshire. Originally from Portland, ME, Alexander earned his BS from Green Mountain College and his MBA from Franklin Pierce University. He has published work in the European Journal of Sustainable Development Research. Currently, Alexander resides in Jackson, New Hampshire with his wife and their golden retriever, Olaf.

Nicole Cox (Arizona State University)

Nicole Cox is a professionally-trained research assistant and sustainability advocate focused on issues of environmental justice and ethics. Nicole has conducted extensive research on topics such as water policy, human thermal comfort and urban densification, and the justice implications of nuclear power generation. She completed her undergraduate education at Arizona State University, where she obtained dual degrees in Sustainability and Justice Studies.

Sukhmani Singh (Arizona State University)

Sukhmani Singh is a senior at Arizona State University Barrett, the Honors College majoring in Political Science and Sustainability with a concentration in Policy and Governance, minoring in Spanish, and working towards a certificate in Energy & Sustainability. After graduation, she hopes to attend law school and eventually pursue a career in environmental law and energy policy. Currently, she works with a non-profit organization called Solar United Neighbors as a Policy and Advocacy intern where she advocates for the expansion of rooftop solar in Arizona. Outside of school and work, Sukhmani spends her time volunteering with *They See Blue* in an effort to mobilize South Asian-Americans to vote.

Endangered Ecosystems: Rights of Nature Protection for the Benefit of Both Ecosystems and Individual Species

Snowy forest with the Rocky Mountains in the distance. Taken in Boulder, Colorado, USA. (Louise Campbell, 2017)

Foreword

At a time when multiple industry groups, and political factions are attempting to dismantle the Endangered Species Act (ESA) in the United States, it may appear as though this almost 50-year-old law is destined for its own extinction (Davenport, & Friedman, 2018). Many of those against this law see it as simply an impediment to people's livelihoods. Many of those in favor of this law see it as the quintessential law needed to save endangered species still threatened after almost five decades of ESA protection (Howard, 2017).

The arguments presented here, however, point to the ESA as a law that does not go far enough to protect non-human species and that it needs to be purposefully supplemented with new legislation in order to protect entire ecological systems (hereafter referred to as ecosystems) wherein both endangered and non-endangered species live. Therefore, the ESA and other similar laws not only need to stay, but additional legislation is needed in the United States and around the world with all-encompassing ecosystems protection laws that not only protect species at risk, but that ensures the protection of the ecosystems that are home to these species as well as many other species that are not now identified as endangered.

Protection of this kind is needed in order to ensure that the mutually beneficial and yet not fully understood relationships between species and between species and their environment is provided, thereby securing the survival of both.

It is recommended here to accomplish this bjy using a "Rights of Nature" (RoN) approach in which entire ecosystems and the components of ecosystems are guaranteed the right to life under international and national law. This kind of change calls into use a systems thinking approach as opposed to the reductionist thinking of saving just one species here and another species somewhere else. The long-term benefits for natural systems and human societies are shown to be better served with a comprehensive approach that emphasizes the need to protect that which is known and that which may never be known about any of these highly complex ecosystems.

Chapter 1

Introduction

View of a lake with the Rocky Mountains beyond.
Yellowstone National Park, Wyoming, USA (Amber
Leversedge 2015)

Environmental justice advocates have for
decades stressed the need for a more holistic
approach to ecological system (ecosystem)
protection, predicated on more respect for

everything from non-human animals to bodies of water. For the purposes of this study, ecosystems are defined as follows: "An ecosystem is comprised of all the non-living elements and living species in a specific local environment. Components of most ecosystems include water, air, sunlight, soil, plants, microorganisms, insects and animals. Ecosystems may be terrestrial – that is, on land – or aquatic" (Harris, 2018, para 1).

This kind of justice advocacy follows the thinking of philosophers such as Aldo Leopold with his land ethic approach giving humans the moral responsibility to protect the land, for the land's sake, and with a focus on healthy, self-renewing ecosystems (Leopold, 1949).

While this 70-year old line of reasoning may still represent a outlying concept to some, the current state of climate change and the continued human-caused environmental degradation of ecosystems worldwide provides abundant evidence for the need for a plethora of healthy land ecosystems and water ecosystems as well. Numerous countries have already taken steps to address more widespread ecosystem protection, yet the means by which these measures are implemented and enforced vary greatly.

The differing success of existing programs and laws aimed at greater ecosystem protection begs the question of how to most effectively "speak for the non-human," (White, 2014, pg. 44) in a way that not only expresses the vitality of ecosystems to human life but also captures their intrinsic value in non-anthropogenic terms. This book will explore ethics and justice in ecosystem protection through first examining the role of justice in the natural world, followed by an analysis of the concept of Rights of Nature and a look at instances where ethics and justice have worked in the favor of natural ecosystems in comparison to unethical environmental practices.

These analyses will inform a final discussion of potential pathways to ethical ecosystem protection, supported by accounts by sustainability and justice experts and inspired by the ideas of environmentalists such as Aldo Leopold, Peter Singer, and Paul W. Taylor, in order to argue that Rights of Nature and environmental justice principles can be utilized more holistically to create systems of ethical ecosystem protection.

Chapter 2

The U.S. Endangered Species Act – A Historical Perspective

View of the San Francisco Bay, California, USA (Louise Campbell 2017)

The 1973 Endangered Species Act enacted in the United States was a landmark law that was passed at a time when there was a turning point in the attitudes and realizations of many of the American people. As a result of postwar industrial progression, the negative externalities of a robust economy were leading to severe environmental degradation (Andersen, 2007). Environmental systems that were previously robust enough to withstand the level of environmental harm being done by the mechanisms of industrial progress were being recognized as being under attack. Rachel Carson's book Silent Spring had been published in 1962, however, her warnings of the consequences of unrestrained industrial practices were still not the mainstream position of the time.

Key areas of this uptick in negative environmental externalities were the increased use of industrial chemicals in a post war agrarian food system; increased levels of pollution from recently improved production systems created to support the war effort; and an expansion of consumption, made possible by the unprecedented levels of product creation as a result of a mechanized industrial system to support the last world war, and increased levels of economic commerce, investment, and globalization (Andersen, 2007; Hawken, 2010). Business and economics were doing well, although, after some time the negative externalities associated with this progress began to show their effects on the natural world. Shortly after Carson's publication, however, and as a result of popular counter-culture thinking, a new consensus was developing that America's relationship with the natural world had reached a point in which the need to conquer, expand, and control needed to shift to an attitude of protection, conservation, and stewardship.

Limits to the amount of strain that the system of the natural world could burden were being found; and they were being represented by smog, acid rain, pesticide poisonings, polluted waterways, deforestation and declining wildlife populations, among other detrimental human and environmental impacts.

During this period - between the early 1960s and the mid 1970s - many federal laws were passed to curb the amount of environmental damage being done as a result of industrial progress. These new laws helped to outline an objective of redefining human relationships with the natural world, and reconciling with these limits of natural capital, and in effect forcing industry to abide by regulations in order to project the macro commons that everyone shared.

The Clean Air Act of 1963, the Wilderness Act of 1964, and the Clean Water Act of 1972, were all aimed at the reduction of environmental pollutants, and the protection of natural ecosystems. New federal departments, like the Environmental Protection Agency (created in 1970) ensured a body of active personnel to manage and oversee the compliance of these laws. Combined with private organizations, not for profit groups, and NGOs, a large galvanized network of environmentally conscious individuals help steer the future to a position of healthier ecosystems, and an economy that can both lead the world without relying on an unsustainable relationship with the natural capital on which it was dependent upon. These changes combined with previous environmental laws, the formation of the EPA and a favorable governing body all led to the 1973 Endangered Species Act.

Chapter 3

Strengths and Weaknesses of the Endangered Species Act

A snowy plain with the Rocky Mountains in the distance.
Taken in Boulder, Colorado, USA (Louise Campbell, 2017)

Since its inception, the Endangered Species Act (ESA) has widely been viewed as a success. Few can argue that the act hasn't pushed the value of environmental conservation into the forefront of the American consciousness. The positive impacts of the act are self-evident with the statistics of animal stewardship.

Moreover, the endangered species act has cemented itself in name recognition across the country. From the ubiquitous elementary school report project, to the popular charitable campaigns using the charismatic megafaunas known to be on the ESA list, it seems that environmental conservation and the ESA work together hand in glove. Criticisms of the act can be found in the details of the regulation. Not unlike economic policies that can be fraught with perverse incentives, negative externalities, loopholes, and misleading progress hidden behind a veil of statistical tradecraft; the ESA's mission is having unintended negative consequences.

A 3.5% Success Rate

As of May of 2018, there were 1,459 animals and 949 plants on the endangered species list that were either listed as threatened or endangered. For the purposes of this paper, the focus is on the data relating to only the species classified as animals. Since 1973, 84 species have been removed from the list. Of those 84 species, 53 of them have been categorized as recovered. 11 of the 84 have been listed as extinct, and the remaining 20 were removed for reasons of error, or technical reclassification. By taking the current number of species, and adding the number of recovered species, plus the number of extinct species, one can summarize the total list of species that have been on the list - 1,523. From that number, the number of recovered species is calculated from the original number of species that were truly endangered or threatened - approximately 3.5%. See Table 1, below.

Table 1 ESA Listed animal and plant species numbers as of May, 2018.

Listed Animal Species	Listed Plant Species
1,459	949
Delisted Recovered	84 53
Extinct	11
Original Data In Error. Not Listed	4
Taxonomic Revision	8
New Information Discovered	6
Act Amendment	1
Erroneous Data	1

This type of statistical calculation could be used to argue that the act itself is not fully functional, if over a 40-year historical observation period, a species has a 3.5% chance of being removed from the list and recovered. Although there are many optics with which one can look at these statistics; a few points can be made with relative confidence.

1.) The chances of coming off the endangered species list once being placed on it are small.

2.) The number of species that have been categorized as "recovered", compared to the overall number of species on the list is small.

Importantly – while the ESA has protected certain key species, it has done little in the way of protecting large numbers of creatures that are not at the time considered to be a species that is threatened or endangered. One critical example has to do with insects of all kinds. By some estimates, between 70% and 80% of all flying insects by biomass have vanished across the globe from just 1994 to 2016 (Hallmann, et. al., 2017). This Hallmann study was conducted in Germany, however, others have chimed in with similar results across the globe. The graph below indicates the mass of flying insects captured in the German study dropping by 78% in just over a few decades (see Figure 1). A massive loss of insects such as this not only demonstrates the ineffectiveness of protecting just certain threatened or endangered species, but it also presents an argument that given the enormous number of insect species being affected, that species by species protection is impractical.

We may find ourselves protecting a few unique butterfly species here and there while all of the other thousands of other species of butterflies, moths, wasps, bees, flies, ants, sawflies, grasshoppers, crickets and so on are found to be suddenly missing. Given that there are literally millions of insect species, the logistics of trying to incorporate even a small percentage of them into the ESA demonstrates on its own, the fallacy of using the ESA as the preferred tool to stave off the looming extinction of so many insects.

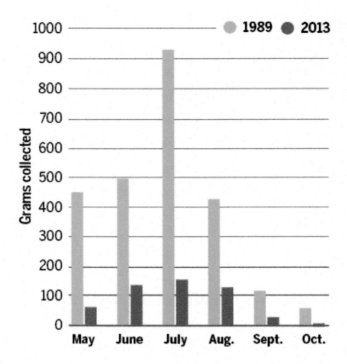

Figure 1 – GRAPHIC) G. GRULLÓN/*SCIENCE*; (DATA) M. SORG *ET AL.*, MITTEILUNGEN AUS DEM ENTOMOLOGISCHEN VEREIN KREFELD 1, 1–5 (2013) © 2013 ENTOMOLOGISCHER VEREIN KREFELD – Vogel (2017).

And yet, given the services of the millions of insect species in steep decline across the globe, it is clear that something needs to be done to protect them from whatever the causes are that are leading to such a sharp decline in numbers. Insects interact with essentially all land-based ecosystems as food providers, decomposers, pest controllers, pollinators, and as soil transformers.

Similar roles are found in water systems as well. Their losses immediately impact other species that depend on these services ranging from other insects to birds to humans. Further massive worldwide insect loss, in fact, may cause human societies to collapse into chaos as well as the living world as it is known today (Kolbert, 2020).

The causes of these losses are at present believed to be habitat loss, pesticide use, herbicide use, other industrial outputs, climate change and in essence – expanding human activities. But even though scientists do not know precisely what actions have led to this enormous loss of insects, particularly flying insects, it is known that insects will find ways to exist and eke out a living if they are just given land, space and plants to live on. The argument for protecting lands, lakes, rivers and even ocean systems therefore, is one both of prevention against the unknown and one based on the knowledge of what works.

These "apocalyptic" insect losses also point to the need to change farming practices to end the use of herbicide and insecticide use completely, moving to organic farming methods and other well-established environmentally friendly practices. These practices include regenerative farming techniques, restoration of abandoned farmlands, perma-gardening, practicing agroforestry, silvo-pasturing, tree intercropping, and conservation agriculture which are all ways to improve the environmental health of agricultural projects while also providing suitable habitat for flying insects such as pollinator species.

Coincidently, these practices mentioned are also valuable CO_2 drawdown methods as outlined in the book Drawdown (Hawken, 2017). Solutions such as these point to the need for holistic and ecocentric approaches and away from the predominant reductionistic and anthropocentric approaches of the present such as are integral to commercial farming and livestock practices.

Chapter 4

Shoot, Shovel and Shut Up - Perverse Incentives

Trees populate a crater in the Craters of the Moon National Park, Idaho, USA (Amber Leversedge, 2015)

Shoot, Shovel, and Shut Up is a colloquial phrase known to (mostly rural) landowners who observe an endangered species on their property and recognize it for the amount of restriction and regulation that falls on landowners once such a species is also observed by conservation workers. This concept takes root in the notion that although a species may be endangered or threatened, their value as a species is less than that of the value of the land use that a private landowner is looking to gain.

There can be several reasons for a disparity in this value. An endangered species may be a predator and be a threat to a landowner's livestock - and therefore a threat to a landowner's personal revenue (Taus, 2016). An endangered species established habitat on a landowner's property may preclude a land development project that is planned. By stopping such a project, the value of the land could go down, again removing revenue from the landowner's pocket. As a result of situations like these, landowners (acting as rational actors with regard to their own self-interest), may choose to remove - kill - the species, remove noticeable evidence of their existence, and move forward with their land-use plan.

Situations like these are called perverse incentives. It happens when an economic policy has an ironic turn of events and actually acts against the intended core purpose of the intended policy. That is to say, that in situations like these the endangered species in question is actually more endangered since their protection plan becomes at odds with the livelihood of others.

When accounting for the relationships like the ones between landowners and endangered species, a systemic approach could be more advantageous, since it would view the landowner's incentives into the policy creation, likely arriving at a more advantageous outcome - for example, income restoration as a result of loss of property value. By taking the ownership of the land away from the land-owner, the perverse incentive is removed and any endangered species on a given piece of land are less likely to be killed for economic reasons.

One thing that both sides can agree on, whether a party is in support of the ESA and believes that it's a structure of providing an adequate amount of measurable good; or whether the belief is there are aspects of the act that are short cited, and there is room for improvement to enhance the positive effects that it produces, there is undoubted value in the presence of strong federal regulation to act as a guiding hand to protect the natural world that is under assault from a world that at times seems to choose to think there is a qualitative difference between human beings and the other creatures who share this planet.

Chapter 5

Natural Systems Exemplars

A clear lake reflects the surrounding mountains in Boulder,

Colorado, USA (Louise Campbell, 2017)

Natural systems provide numerous untold benefits to non-humans and humans alike. Any natural system, in fact, is a highly complex system of interconnected species in which each species contributes to the system in ways those knowledgeable in such as ecologists, biologists, botanists, soil scientists, and other experts will be the first to admit they know very little about. This general lack of understanding is one important reason to preserve these systems if there is to be any hope of duplicating them in the future and as future civilizations needs dictate. Once they are gone, there is no way to put them back together again and the information on what and why they existed is lost in perpetuity. Beyond this need, though, these systems need to be preserved for the many interconnected services they provide to both non-human and human species.

Small Systems

Some natural systems can be so small so as to completely escape attention, and yet many species will still call these places home and will exist there.

Even a puddle can constitute an ecosystem (Harris, 2018). Or, something as non-descript as a hedgerow adjacent to farmland can provide a much-needed home for several plant, insect and animal species. Kolbert (2020) describes one such place in an old irrigation ditch next to a 1, 300-acre farm in Stockton, California. This hedgerow that extends for roughly a half kilometer, that was planted with a variety of shrubs such as white sage, elderberry and Woods' rose is home to a myriad of insects such as leaf-cutter bees and sweat bees that in turn attract other species such as several bird species. What is remarkable is how this tiny ecosystem can exist adjacent to commercial farmland, and yet it does. In this case, all it took for this system to establish itself here was for the farmer to not plow every inch of the available land, to leave hedgerows around the periphery, and to allow life to find these precious islands of living space. "We have lots of data that show if you do this, they will come" (Kolbert, 2020, p. 65). Similarly, to the expression "If you build it, they will come", with natural systems it appears that "If we allow it, they will come".

An Urban Park

As another example of how small natural systems can exist and coexist with heavily impacted environments, consider a small illustration in the NW, U.S., of Orchard Park in Hillsboro, Oregon. This park consists of over twenty acres of primarily natural vegetation with similarities to temperate forest areas around the globe. And although this urban park consists of several ecosystems within it such as a wetland area, a temperate forest area, and a creek named Rock Creek, it can be protected as one entity and easily identified with a conveniently established boundary due to the housing and industrial communities surrounding it.

This small forested space displays many shades of green, with some trees over a hundred and fifty feet tall, contains a lush understory, and has Rock Creek meandering throughout. The top story consists of Douglas firs, western red cedars, western hemlock, Oregon ash, cottonwoods, red alders, several maple species, poplars, white oak, and even a few Colorado blue spruce trees. The understory is full of vine maples, Oregon grape, sword and bracken ferns, red huckleberry bushes, salmonberry bushes, thick grass in places over three feet high, rhododendrons, ocean spray, salal, a few western trillium flowers, and several other species. The park's wetlands are just as diverse with tall wetland grasses in places, several wildflower species, western crabapple, western red cedars mixed in the grassy areas, dogwoods, blue and red elderberry, cattails, skunk cabbage, and several other species.

In short, there is a lot of variety and complexity in this small park. Much of which is not adequately described here. The soil types and chemistry, for example, vary significantly throughout this park depending on whether the samples taken are in the wetland, in the forest, in the grassy areas, along the riparian areas of the creek or in other places.

It would seem, in fact that all of the species in the park exhibit different forms of collaboration with other species, with competition for space acting as an antecedent to this collaboration. Markedly, the collaboration observed among these plant species and the insect and animal species is worth discussion and how this kind of collaboration may pertain to human systems and human interactions. In addition, many of the plant species within this park are only suitable for certain soil types and specific sunlight exposure as well as water needs. The whole system, in fact, demonstrates complexity, interdependence, and interconnectedness. Some species appear to depend absolutely on just one other species while others appear to need several and even all of the species in order to survive.

Endangered species such as the western white trillium in this park or the federally protected red tail hawk both call this park home and either can be threatened with seemingly small disruptions in any part of this park. The hawks, in fact, frequent all parts of this park, making them particularly vulnerable to human activities such as the use of herbicides and pesticides.

Several of these park genera it seems, appear to repeat processes and perform singular tasks on a grand scale. As an example, the Douglas fir trees here produce a prodigious amount of brown ~ 2" (5 cm) long female seed cones (by the hundreds respectively) each year, in addition to thousands more respectively of the smaller reddish male pollen cones that are only about a quarter-inch (0.63 cm) long. The female cones tend to fall in late autumn and winter and the male cones disperse themselves on the ground for several months after they produce yellowish pollen in the spring. The makeup of male cones that fall to the ground is so concentrated in places that it looks like the ground has been covered with a thick layer of bark dust.

The effect is a blanket of reddish hue pollen cones on the forest floor. The female cones are abundant in places too, as many as two-dozen per square meter under the trees. Each of these seed cones produces hundreds of seeds, and yet interestingly, with this seemingly massive effort at reproduction, only a handful of Douglas fir seedlings are found in this entire park. This reproduction effort, which is prolific but appears to be anything but precise, is found to be beneficial throughout the ecosystem, even though the benefit for the fir trees is not that obvious.

The squirrels, field mice, chipmunks, sparrows, finches, chickadees and other species all depend on these fir tree seeds as an important part of their diet, particularly in the winter months. In fact, it would appear that all of these creatures' benefit to some extent, and yet it appears to be at the expense of the Douglas fir tree. The trees do benefit from the nutrient-rich droppings of several of these animals and particularly from the Douglas squirrel and the Townsend chipmunk that reportedly disperse essential fungi and bacteria needed by these trees (Carey, 1991).

Another critical source of nutrition for these trees comes from the tree lichen, which releases much needed nitrogen into the soil after falling from the tree branches. It is surprising, though, that with tens of thousands of cones and millions of seeds dispersed each year that there are not more Douglas fir seedlings here. And this is just one example of many other such patterns of species reproduction efforts in this forest, similar to the cottonwood, maple tree, Oregon ash trees, and species. Little is known as to why there is such redundancy in a system such as this, but it is clear that many other species within and without this system benefit as a result. Certainly, humans benefit from the oxygen produced by these fir trees and the other vegetation and human society benefits from the clean air and water provided by environments such as these. Some other benefits tend to be less tangible, such as the peace, tranquility, and the aesthetic beauty afforded by environments such as these.

Many species in a forest such as this, in fact, contribute to the whole of the ecosystem in a collaborative and seemingly communal way. This occurs with animals, birds, insects and the native fauna. Several native bees, for example, provide much needed pollination along with bumblebees, several fly species and other pollinators such as Anna's hummingbirds, various butterflies, mosquitos, and moths. The Douglas fir trees produce prodigious amounts of nutrients to the forest floor that over time contribute to other essential organisms such as fungi. These nutrients benefit other trees and plants, and these actions combined with several other processes create a living habitat for many other plants as well as for many animals. The red tree vole, moreover, depends entirely on the Douglas fir tree for its existence, living primarily on the needles from these trees. Other species, in turn, such as the northern and the great horned owl depend on the voles as a source of food and depend on the lichen produced in these trees for their nesting needs (Carey, 1991).

A similar pattern of millions of seeds, flowers, and leaf dispersal processes is repeated over and over in this small park, from one season to another, as well as in all forest ecosystems. The seeds, cones, tree bark and all of the fir needles all provide essential nutrients for the understory trees, bushes, grasses and wetland species. The lichen falling from the trees provides for the advantage of any plant that happens to be in its vicinity. In the understory, other animals such as Willamette brush bunnies, common garter snakes, and Oregon chipmunks make full use of the fallen debris for both habitat and as cover from predators such as coyotes and great horned owls. Many other species, both animal and plant, benefit from each other with the aid of the continual replenishment of needed organic material to the forest floor for the use of following generations—with a span of decades, even centuries into the future. This, therefore, is a long-term effort ongoing within this ecosystem that has benefits accumulating over time as opposed to degrading over time. All of these trees and other foliage nutrients are working in combination with countless insects, animals, and microorganisms. With all of these concurrent processes happening over time, the soil changes, resulting in rich organic topsoil, more suitable for germination and thus for future generations. This whole process, which may seem overly redundant to us, reveals that natural systems tend to be inexact, generous, long term oriented—and that they pave the way for the needs of others in the future.

What immediately stands out to even a casual observer in a place such as this, is the shear variety of species present. Many different insects and birds are seen here without much effort, whilst these same life forms are not often seen just hundreds of feet outside of this urban park. It would seem, therefore, that no matter how hostile and unforgiving the environment is just outside of an ecosystem such as this, that various life forms are drawn here and even manage to eke out a living in this urban area within this isolated and somewhat diverse patch of living space. And this may be the most important point to be made here. Animal and insect species come to these isolated patches of land because of the vegetation afforded them and because of other reasons such as the absence of pesticides and other motivations or unknown benefits. And they come here to live despite the human influences occurring all around them.

Looking at the whole, it is clear that the system functions well, even if there is a lack of understanding as to why or a comprehension of all of the intricate processes contained within. Arguably, a holistic approach to understanding natural systems is preferred if one wishes to have a better understanding of the patterns, and the long-term strategies. Just as importantly, it should also be clear that natural systems themselves have a strategy and a plan, best viewed with a holistic perspective as opposed to examining singled out species or small areas of an ecosystem. This is not to say that natural systems are sentient systems, per se, just that there does appear to be a plan in place that unfolds over time, with long term benefits for the whole of the system. A holistic and systems approach to understanding natural systems affords the needed perspective of order that may counter a perspective of a chaotic interaction when viewed on a smaller scale (Wells, 2013). When, in fact, every ecosystem has a balance of its own, with a certain number of each variety balancing certain numbers of other varieties, some dependent upon one another, some competing for similar food sources and all dependent on the integrity and completeness of the ecosystem as a whole.

This one example of a small ecosystem should help with the appreciation that there are many processes that lead to the long-term health of a system such as this and that these systems are highly complex, with many species competing for a given space or niche. In addition to competing for space, however, there is just as much collaboration and even cooperation between species, all contributing to systems that often flourish and that tend to confound those who wish to understand the whole by dissecting the parts.

The need, therefore, is to protect all species within an ecosystem, endangered and non-endangered alike for the sake of preserving the complexity within and for the essential services provided to humans.

Humankind simply may never understand enough about the complex processes contained within any given system, and yet it is known that by protecting a natural living habitat, those species that use that habitat are protected. Therefore, protecting an entire ecosystem provides multiple advantages for us. This not only protects all of the species within, but it protects the knowledge needed should these systems need to be duplicated later or should a better understanding of the processes be needed as they pertain to systems such as these.

A natural system like this also points to the need for active management for many such systems in order to protect the whole of the system.

Invasive species such as English ivy, reed canary grass, and Himalayan blackberries are threatening many of the native species in this system. This small ecosystem is also threatened by insects such as the Japanese beetle that is actively infesting and threatening many plant species here.

On an even smaller scale – some of the western red cedars are succumbing to the didymascella thujina fungus. All of these threats and more have been introduced by humans due to the proximity to adjacent neighborhoods. Just as importantly, however, all of these threats can benefit from human intervention to either remove them or to treat them. These ecosystems in close proximity to civilization, in particular, need continual, close, hands-on intervention for the health needs of the whole ecosystem. These urban systems need active and ongoing management.

Larger Systems

It has been asserted, and the argument is supported here that the entire planet Earth is one large ecosystem. The prospect of this kind of labeling, however, is daunting to the average conservationist minded proponent and may even be counter-productive to the needs to protect the many ecosystems within the larger Earth ecosystem because it frames the problems and responsibilities as being overwhelmingly large. Even so, this labeling does indicate that humans too are part of this larger system and this helps define humankind's role in the many large and small ecosystems contained within the Earth ecosystem as a whole.

Another concern with this kind of gargantuan labeling of ecosystems is that the human impacts, both positive and negative tend to get lost in the size and complexity of the problem. It is difficult to define the boundaries needed for modern-day problem solving with this kind of labeling.

By the same token, it is still quite necessary for to see Earth as one large ecosystem in order to address ecosystem challenges holistically using systems thinking approaches for problem solving. It is also necessary to be conscious of the bigger picture and the reality that all ecosystems are intrinsically connected to one another with continual interactions happening on a moment by moment basis.

Before continuing with larger ecosystem examples, it is helpful here to revisit the definition of an ecosystem. "An ecosystem consists of all the living and non-living things in a specific natural setting. Plants, animals, insects, microorganisms, rocks, soil, water and sunlight are major components of many ecosystems. All types of ecosystems fall into one of two categories: terrestrial or aquatic. Terrestrial ecosystems are land-based, while aquatic are water-based" (Harris, 2018, para 12). And it is also important to note that no two ecosystems of the same type are really the same, each having different species and each consisting of unique water or soil chemistry as well as unique inputs such as variable light from the sun or the influences from other adjacent ecosystems. Each distinct type of an ecosystem is also known as a biome.

Within the parent Earth ecosystem, there are a myriad of small to very large ecosystems, including some with categorical types and some as of yet to still be labeled. A few of these well-identified ecosystems are as follows (Harris, 2018):

- Tropical Rainforest Ecosystems. These are located in tropical regions near the equator consisting of a great diversity of both plant and animal life. Noted as having a greater variety of animal and plant life as compared to any other type of ecosystem. As much as fifty percent of the plant species found in the world are found in tropical rainforests (Nix, 2019). These plants serve a myriad of purposes with one very important purpose of providing gas exchanges and oxygen for animals. Tropical rainforests also contain more animal species than any other ecosystem with insects making up the largest percent.

- Temperate Forest Ecosystem. Often consisting of deciduous trees as well as coniferous trees in temperate climates with cold winters and warm summers. A few of the many coniferous trees found in these systems include coastal redwood trees, Douglas fir, ponderosa pine and western red cedar. Deciduous trees include many forms of maple tree, alders, oak and dogwood (ASU, n.d.).

- Taiga Ecosystems. Sometimes referred to as boreal forests and found in the far northern regions, just south of the Arctic. Primarily consisting of coniferous trees such as spruce, fir, hemlock and pine. These forests are found in the northern latitudes of 50 degrees to 60 degrees north and to the south of tundra biomes further to the north (Nelson, 2020).

- Grassland Ecosystems. Treeless systems or with sparse trees with grasses in semi-arid areas with sub-categories such as savannas found in the tropics, and prairies found in temperate regions. About half of all of Africa is covered by savanna as well as large areas of Australia, South America and India. Savannas are characterized by dry conditions up to four months of the year with rainfall between 20 and 50 inches per year in the wetter months and by highly porous soils. Temperate grasslands such as the prairies of North America and the veldts of South Africa also have grasses as the dominant vegetation but have moderate rainfall and cold winters in addition to hot summers (UCMP, 2020a).

- Desert Ecosystems. Relatively sparse vegetation and in drier areas than grasslands, although not always hot and they are also found in temperate zones as well as cold areas and coastal areas. These biomes cover as much as one fifth of the Earth with ground features that vary from rocky to sandy to gravelly and animal populations that are sparse. The species that do occupy this kind of an ecosystem have special adaptations to live in these dry conditions. As examples, reptile species are dominant in these biomes and the mammal species tend to be quite small such as the kangaroo mice in North American deserts (UCMP, 2020b).

- Tundra Ecosystems. These are treeless systems as well located in polar regions or on the tops of high mountains that are snow for the most of the year. Typically, cold and windy and often frozen all year long. During the brief warmer months, snow melt may expose small vegetation such as wildflowers and lichens. Animals may include marmots, sheep, mountain goats and several bird species. The species that do live in these harsh environments are stressed by the conditions, barely clinging to life and as such, highly susceptible to environmental disturbances (Nunez, 2019).

- Stillwater Ecosystems. Examples include lakes, bogs, springs, ponds, bays, swamps, marshes and lagoons. Often with floating plants and underwater plants as well as others that inhabit calm waters. Several of these water systems are freshwater systems, such as rivers, lakes, springs and ponds but there are also salt marshes and saltwater swamps in addition to freshwater marshes and freshwater swamps. Lagoons are typically saltwater systems separated from the larger saltwater body such as an ocean by a land mass such as a shoal or a bar. Bays and/or estuaries are typically brackish water. Estuaries are highly productive ecosystems and are found where freshwater from a river or stream meets the ocean and can be called a bay, lagoon, slough or sound (EPA, 2020).

- River and Stream Ecosystems. Moving freshwater systems such as streams and rivers are characterized by higher oxygen content due to the turbulence created as opposed to still-water systems. This higher oxygen content allows for a higher biodiversity as compared to still-water systems as well.

These freshwater systems are often created by springs or melting ice and ultimately empty into lakes or oceans. Plant species include mosses, submerged plants and algae and may also contain emergent plants such as cattails and flowering rush. These biomes also contain many species of fish as well as amphibians, invertebrates and even exotic species such as alligators, crocodiles, and hippopotamus (Faucheux, 2017).

- Littoral Zones. These are sometimes referred to as intertidal zones and are found on ocean coastlines, and are shallow marine saltwater systems near the shoreline with high turbulence due to the wave action. These systems can also display a high degree of biodiversity with seaweed, kelp, seagrass, and often including, mollusks, oysters, barnacles, and many forms of crustacean species. Estuaries also fall within the littoral zone. Ocean littoral zones tend to be inhospitable environments because of the constant change leading to temporary conditions. Intertidal zones are further broken down into spray zones, high intertidal, middle intertidal and low intertidal zones (NOAA, 2020a).

- Coral Reefs. Very high diversity systems liken in biodiversity to tropical rainforests. The identifying namesake inhabitant is the coral polyps which is an invertebrate sessile (lacking self-locomotion) organism that relies on its relationship with a plant-like algae. Coral structures, which are derived from thousands of different coral species, constitute the largest biologically originated structures on the planet. With as many as one-quarter of all marine life depending on them to some degree. These are typically shallow water systems consisting of many crustacean species along with corals, sponges, sea anemones, and many fish species. There are also deep-sea corals as well which rely on plankton for their energy needs as opposed to photosynthesis (NOAA, 2020b)

- Other Marine Ecosystems. Those marine systems that are not coral reefs, or littoral zones or landlocked systems such as lagoons and marshes - up to and including the vast open sea. With life forms ranging from sharks to sea turtles, tuna, rays, octopus, squids, sea cucumbers, whales, dolphins, jellyfish, shrimp, countless medium to large fish species and vast numbers of smaller species such as sardines, krill and anchovies. The open ocean is also brimming with the very small but highly important algae and phytoplankton life that are at the bottom of this biome's food chain. Occupying 71% of the planet's surface, this open ocean system consists of three main zones of: the upper, the middle zone and the deep zone. Each of these zones are characterized as having different light conditions and with unique life forms contained within (Oceana, 2020).

All of these types of ecosystems are unique and yet inter-connected with one another with commonalities such as sharing the gases in the atmosphere and water being shared throughout all of the systems.

The protection designation of these ecosystems can be based on pre-determined ecosystem geographic identifiers such as has been placed on well-established maps, or as identified by the portions within the boundaries of nations and states.

In addition, their identified geographical boundary of protection can extend beyond the ecosystems themselves to include other ecosystems in order to ensure connectivity conservation across ecosystem boundaries. This later case, in fact, has been practiced widely with examples including Marine Protected Areas (MPA) and Wilderness Areas

(WA). Most MPAs and WAs consist of multiple ecosystems contained within. It can be argued, in fact, that protected areas such as these have advantages over just protecting a given ecosystem because with multiple ecosystems involved, this allows for inter-ecosystems connectivity conservation and all of the complex interactions that occur within and between ecosystems. The protection of the intrinsic life of a given ecosystem, though, mandates that all of each ecosystem contained within an MPA or a WA be included as part of that protected area. As an example, an MPA or a combination of connected MPAs would need to include all of a designated coral reef for the needed protection of that specific ecosystem.

Given the varieties of ecosystems, the interconnections between ecosystems and the added layers of human imposed ownership boundaries, it is apparent that the protection of some ecosystems are comparatively straight-forward as compared to the protection of others. A lake ecosystem, for example, will have a well-established boundary from which to identify as an area on a map that needs to be protected from human interference. This will naturally include the whole of the lake and the riparian zones adjacent to the lake all around the perimeter of the lake. Establishing the geographical boundary for an open ocean ecosystem, on the other hand, brings with it the difficulty of determining just what the outer boundaries of that system are, the added need to protect all of the zones of that system while also contending with the geographical boundaries of the nation or nations maritime boundaries.

Chapter 6

The Fallacy of Selecting One or a Few Species Within a System

Grazing elk in Boulder, Colorado, USA (Louise Campbell, 2017)

The ecosystems described above are indicative of the variability of a wide variety of ecosystems. Although these descriptions do not go into the great depths of understanding needed in the disciplines studying these systems, they do provide at least a glimpse of the species variety potential and the complexity of these systems.

A soil scientist, for example, would go into much greater detail concerning the many soil types in a system and would offer a better understanding of the sheer volume as well as variety of microbial life in land-based systems. Millions of microbes in a single gram of soil and thousands of species in that same gram, all providing important functions and many in a symbiotic relationship with the plants using this soil. A soil scientist would caution that if it were not for certain soil types and specific soil chemistry, the flora species that do live there, would not exist and would be replaced by other, more suitable species. In the end, they argue, it is the soil chemistry that determines which species exist and which do not exist in a given land system.

Soil scientists, as it turns out, are also one of the groups of scientists to remind others that they know very little about the vast complexity of a given system and that very slight changes will deselect one plant species and select others. A slight change in the pH of the soil or the dominance of one microbial species over another will inhibit some species from growing and encourage others to grow. Added to this, the knowledge needed to alter the soil chemistry sufficiently in one direction or another is still out of their grasp, and most attempts at designing ecosystems with the limited knowledge available today end up being exercises in futility. Nature, as it turns out, will decide on its own which species live where, and not humans. Sure, certain species can be planted, but that does not mean they will still be there just a few years later. They may be outcompeted by other plants, selectively eaten by herbivores, prone to disease, intolerant of the precipitation levels, or simply not be able to exist with the given soil conditions. In many such attempts at designing ecosystems –a "designed ecosystem" years later will become an entirely new system with none of the species purposefully introduced there and instead filled with unintended interlopers. Because these volunteers were selected by natural processes, however, their chances of survival are far greater than if they had been artificially introduced by humans.

This same natural selection process applies across all ecosystems. The same principle of selection applies, in fact, with attempts at protecting just one species or another in a given ecosystem. The desire may be, for example, try to protect a certain raptor bird species, which is both a keystone species and an apex species at the top of the ecological food chain. That attempt, nevertheless, may not take into consideration the needs of the ecosystem or ecosystems this species needs as a habitat. There are other species within an ecosystem that the raptor, and any other species depends upon and if they are not also protected then the raptor cannot survive there. This argument of inter-species dependency helps to make the case for ecosystem protection as opposed to single species protection. A single species needs an ecosystem for survival and therefore the most effective means for protecting one species or another is the protection of the ecosystem(s) they depend upon for survival.

The loss of an unprotected species such as field mice in a given ecosystem will make the survival for a given raptor species more difficult. Given time, however, a protected ecosystem would allow for and even draw these same field mice to return or other prey species the raptor depends upon, but the system needs to be intact in order for this natural progression to occur. Therefore, what is called for is a holistic approach to safeguarding an ecosystem and, as needed, providing ecosystem intervention in the way of management practices in order to maintain the integrity of a given ecosystem. To allow for natural processes to take place, a healthy ecosystem will allow the return of prey species needed for raptor survival.

The interconnectedness of ecosystems and the complexity of interspecies dependencies within any ecosystem must be taken into account with a full appreciation granted for all of the unknowns applying to questions that are both known and unknown. In any given ecosystem several species will be dependent upon other species, the water, the soil, the plants and a host of interactions that are unknown.

Plant species, for example not only depend on the soil chemistry for their niche survival but these plants can change the chemistry either for their own benefit or to thwart competition from others. As an example, several conifer tree species increase the acidity of the soil due to the deposition of their lignin rich needles onto the soil, thereby reducing their competition from many deciduous tree species that are intolerant of low pH soils (Yale, 2020). This is particularly true in boreal forests, and is also true in many temperate forests as well. These predominant conifer tree forests then provide for the needs of other species that depend on the trees themselves or on understory plant species finding their own niche as well as the myriad of mammal, amphibian and insect species all being drawn to these ecosystems dominated by conifer forests.

Protecting the entire ecosystem not only counters the tendency for reductionist thinking but it allows each system to do what they do best, and that is to survive and thrive. As an example, the Aspen ecosystem, a.k.a. Pando forest, at the Fishlake National Forest in Utah, arguably the largest single living organism on the planet, is now dying due to faltered human intervention.

Park management actions combined with adherence to federal regulations have resulted in deer and cattle being allowed to graze in this 100-acre system known as the "Trembling Giant" now call into question the problem of trying to manage forests and wildlife separately (Rogers & McAvoy, 2018). The protection of mule deer under certain hunting regulations is one reason that the deer are allowed to roam around freely in the Pando forest. It has been determined that "within the context of North American aspen, single-species game management has potentially catastrophic effects on a much wider range of plant and animal species which thrive where aspen is intact" (Rogers & McAvoy, 2018, pg. 2).

The problem with the mule deer herbivore grazing, however, is the damage to the aspen suckers caused by the grazing. Cattle tend to do the same kind of damage and even the introduction of predator species such as wolves has done little to thwart the damage caused by both deer and cattle. This ecosystem example, once again, calls for the need to protect entire systems, and to not let any natural system fall prey to the Endangered Species Act or other laws that, although well-intentioned, may result in unintended consequences such as these.

This Aspen ecosystem in Utah underscores the need for not only the protection of an ecosystem by preventing human encroachment on the system, but also the need for active management of systems such as this. Most, if not all, natural ecosystems today are negatively impacted by human influences, both unintentional and intentional. As a result, many of these same ecosystems need active human management in order to negate other negative human influences. These active management practice vary greatly from one system to another, but in the case of this

Aspen ecosystem, the deer and the cattle foraging needs to be controlled. Here, the cattle simply need to be prevented from grazing in the Aspen forest entirely. The mule deer foraging problem, however, is not as simple a problem to solve because these mule deer are native species to the area. It is also true that the high populations of mule deer here can be traced back to human interventions such as the elimination of wolves in this area, the trapping of beavers, or other interventions such as killing off other indigenous grazing species that would be able to compete with the mule deer for foraging needs. Reintroducing wolves in this area, in fact, has been helpful in curtailing the mule deer impact on the Aspens, but has not significantly curtailed the problem of mule deer impact on the ecosystem. The challenges here highlight the need for thoughtful and active management practices that may need to change from year to year and that will need highly qualified professionals who are aware of the ecosystem needs and the number of mule deer a system such as this can tolerate. In other words, the problems encountered in this system help to demonstrate some of the complexities and challenges of addressing human impacts on ecosystems as well as the need for active management as opposed to a hands-off approach to ecosystems protection.

Chapter 7

River Systems

A river flows through a hot spring in Yellowstone National Park, Wyoming, USA (Amber Leversedge 2015)

One of the best examples of the fallacy of trying to protect just this species or that species has to do with dammed rivers and attempts to protect endangered species such as the Coho salmon and other anadromous fish species. Not only do dams prevent aquatic species from moving past them, but by turning portions of rivers into lakes they dramatically alter and segment the river ecosystem.

Lakes are fundamentally different in many ways from rivers. Lakes are thermally stratified, with warmer temperatures at the top and cooler temperatures at the bottom whereas rivers tend to be cooler in general with less stratification. Many aquatic insects and fish are highly sensitive to this alteration in the thermal regime impacting their various life cycles and their ability to live in lakes. These stratification effects in turn affect rivers when either warm water from the top of the lake or cooler water from the bottom of the lake are introduced into the downstream river at different times of the year. These temperature changes to the river vary from summer to winter, but in either case, the water entering the river alters the temperature of the river and impacts the river aquatic life.

Lakes are closed systems, and because of this their chemistry is different than that of a river which is an open ecosystem, exchanging water, heat and matter with its surroundings. Lakes are also lower in dissolve oxygen due to the stillness of the water with deoxygenation occurring because of a lack of oxygen resupply from the surface both because oxygen is less soluble in warm water and because air is not pulled into the water as it is with turbulent rivers (Winton, Calamita & Wehrli, 2019).

In addition, the lower levels of oxygen in lakes leads to anaerobic processes that further alter the chemistry of lake water. Lakes are also prone to eutrophication (richness of nutrients) leading to algae blooms and phytoplankton near the surface (Zartner, 2019). Lakes have higher concentrations of compounds such as hydrogen sulfide as well as reduced iron in the trapped sediment. Put briefly, a river ecosystem ceases to exist once dams are placed in the middle of any given river.

In essence, the stillness of the water in dam created lakes leads to the contamination of the lake water which ultimately leads to the contamination of the downstream river water (McCully, n.d.). This contamination is due to factors such as temperature variances, reduced oxygen, altered acidity, anaerobic decomposition of organic materials, eutrophication impacts and higher concentrations of reduced compounds in trapped sediment behind dams, among other factors.

Sediment trapped behind dams not only contains a concentration of contaminants but the storage of these sediments prevents nutrients from travelling down to the river where it is needed by the river aquatic life. Ironically, this trapped sediment also spells the end of life for instream dams with sediment piling all the way to the top of a dam in as few as 50 to 100 years. The cost of removing this sediment without detrimentally impacting the river downstream of a dam becomes prohibitively expensive once millions of cubic meters of sediment are trapped, ultimately leading to the deconstruction (demolition) of dams.

Added to this, the structural design life of most dams is less than 100 years, meaning they must be demolished or dramatically refurbished after that amount of time, and either replaced with a new dam or not replaced, freeing up the river ecosystem to its previous natural state. Just one example of an instream dam that was demolished due to both its end of life and excessive sediment buildup was the Condit Dam on the White Salmon River in the state of Washington, in the U.S (FWSR, 2020). The removal of this 125-foot high dam in 2011 sent almost 2 million cubic meters of sediment downstream, but opened up over 40 kilometers of White Salmon River habitat for the first time in over 100 years. Now, with the steady healing of this river ecosystem, the survival prospects for the endangered White Salmon River Chinook, the threatened Steelhead trout, the endangered Coho salmon, the bull trout, the lamprey and all of the other aquatic creatures in this ecosystem and all of the land and air creatures interacting with it are significantly improved (FWSR, 2020). In this fairly unique case – the entire river ecosystem has been restored, by the simple act of removing an unnecessary dam, thereby allowing for the return of all the natural interactions and interrelationships between species, both those threatened and those that are not threatened.

The Condit dam did not provide flood control, did not allow for river transportation or allow for fish passage. It was built solely for the purpose of producing electricity. And yet, the maximum generating capacity for this dam of less than 15 MW, can be easily replaced with just 10 average sized wind turbines that do not have the side-effect of completely halting or significantly altering an ecosystem's natural processes.

The inadequacy of fish ladders on dams and the blocked migration caused by dams also points to the delusion of trying to protect certain anadromous fish species as opposed to protecting the entire river ecosystem. In contrast to some recorded accounts, the present-day number of fish successfully navigating instream dams, spawning, and returning to these rivers are as much as two orders of magnitude less than historic, pristine runs (Waldman, 2013).

Most dams, in fact, do not have any kind of fish passage at all, either for upstream travelling adult species or for downstream travelling juvenile fish species. Those few dams that do have fish ladders, are typically hydropower dams that have proven to not only be ineffective for fish migration, but wholly inadequate for any other species migration besides fish. Those dams that do have fish ladders, provide some passage for adult fish travelling upstream but little to no passage for juvenile fish attempting to travel downstream.

Dams on the lower Columbia River and the Snake River in the U.S. Pacific NW, for example, have juvenile bypass systems fitted with holding areas to facilitate transporting juvenile fish downriver either by barges or trucks in order to avoid their dying from nitrogen fixation after travelling through the turbine intakes. The 60 to 70% of the juvenile spring and summer chinook salmon that do avoid the turbines often have to be transported by these artificial means whilst the other 30 to 40% are not so lucky. In all, 15 to 20 million salmon and steelhead juveniles are transported each year by artificial means down these rivers (USACE, 2012). These extraordinary measures at protecting fish species may appear to be ludicrous to some, but even given the inadequacy of these methods, they are superior to the lack of fish protection measures prevalent with many countries around the world. In other words, these efforts on the part of the Corps of Engineers in the Pacific NW of the U.S. are a noble attempt at addressing a desperate and difficult situation created by the presence of instream dams.

Even so, the ongoing pattern of engineering miscalculations, requiring a finned creature, or any other non-human aquatic creature to climb a ladder in order to go upstream further points to the need to restore river ecosystems to their natural state by removing instream dams wherever they exist (Pearce, 2006; Waldman, 2013). The same kind of engineering miscalculation of expecting juvenile finned creatures or any other non-human aquatic creature to recognize the need for and then use a fish ladder or fish elevator to travel downstream highlights both the inadequacy of reductionistic thinking and the wisdom of appreciating a general lack of understanding of how natural systems actually function. The flawed idea of blocking rivers with dams has led to untold examples of environmental and human systems destruction around the planet, including habitat loss, loss of wetlands, loss of cities and villages, loss of natural features such as gorges, forests and waterfalls and the list goes on.

The use of instream dams, in fact, has led to compounded reductionistic engineering solutions that will also seem ludicrous to many, but that again point to the fallacy of engineering inputs into natural systems and the desperate measures taken to protect aquatic species when dams are present. Examples include "fish elevators" and fish passage cooling systems. The fish elevators are to facilitate fish passage across a dam in the same way as a fish ladder although – in this case fish are collected in hoppers and physically lifted up to the lake above a given dam. A fish passage cooling system with "intake chimneys" is meant to be a "temperature improvement system" to aid with issues such as high river water temperature brought on by the presence of the dam and the water restriction caused by the dam. Another example of an artificial system used to facilitate fish movement around a dam is the Lake Billy Chinook fish capture and fish transportation system in Oregon, on this lake formed by the Pelton and Round Butte complex of dams on the Deschutes River. This $62 million-dollar apparatus collects fish in Lake Billy Chinook, separates and sorts them by size and species and then pumps the desired fish via "fish pumps" to trucks so they can be transported downstream. Again, this seems ludicrous to both the casual and the trained observer, but it also represents the kind of noble efforts government agencies such as the Corps of Engineers are willing to experiment with for the sake of certain protected or endangered species.

A simpler and much more effective alternative, however, would be to simply demolish the various hydroelectric dams on the Deschutes River, thereby restoring the ecosystem and the habitat for not just the protected fish species, but for all of the species that benefit from this river.

There are a host of misconceptions with regard to the need for dams, the use of dams, the cost of dams and who is responsible for them once they reach end of life. Large agencies such as the Corps of Engineers, for example, operate on the ongoing principle that dams are necessary, which is rarely the case (Pearce, 2006). Another misconception is that dams are an inexpensive way to produce electricity, which was true several decades ago, before public demands for fish passage for dams, and agencies such as the Corps were forced to find ways to comply with this need. But the cost of retrofitting high head dams with "fish passage engineering" solutions is typically in the hundreds of millions of dollars. As an example – a relatively small project at the Detroit Dam on the North Santiam River in Oregon is expected to cost from $ 100 million to $ 250 million dollars (Poehler, 2018). In fact, the fish passage engineering terms used such as upstream travelling fish ladders, downstream travelling fish ladders, fish elevators, fish escalators, temperature control cooling towers, separate eel ramps, juvenile bypass systems, fish pumps, fish trucks, fish barges, and so on along with the countless options for each, should cause one to pause and to ask why all of this is necessary.

What is the need for the dams in the first place and why only allow for fish to migrate in one direction or another with no regard to any other kinds of aquatic life that all depend on some form of migration in river ecosystem? Not to mention the need for nutrient transport in both directions. The term "fish passage engineering", in fact, should bring into question the very notion that artificial engineering means are going to somehow benefit natural systems.

Granted, arguments for the continued use of instream dams will continue for some time and in some cases, those arguments will seem to be well-founded. These arguments, however, rarely take into account the needs of Nature and do not consider the right of any river system to live for its own sake. Well-founded anthropocentric arguments may be for human drinking water needs and/or irrigation needs for agricultural projects. The fact is that human drinking water needs are a small percentage of the water needed for farming and livestock operations. Much of the water for farming, in fact, ends up being "virtual water" in the form of crop harvests shipped to other countries (Pearce, 2006). And the simple truth is, humanity does not need livestock, ranching and dairy farm operations producing meat and dairy and particularly not in desert environments. Humans fare much better on a plant-based diet anyway and so does the natural world without humans living on an omnivore diet (Hawken, 2017). Neither should agricultural projects be growing water intensive crops or "virtual water" crops in desert environments (Pearce, 2006).

An ecocentric argument, on the other hand, is that the right to life of a given river takes precedence over human civilization needs, and particularly the needs of human civilizations in desert environments. After all, the folly in having large cities in the middle of the desert becomes quite clear when considering the water depletion impacts that human civilizations have on desert environments. And the folly of growing water intensive crops in the middle of the desert or having livestock and dairy operations in the middle of the desert should be even clearer. These practices are short-lived at best, and detrimental to the natural environments that must be tapped into in order to allow for a small extension in time for doomed, short term planning efforts for cities that must eventually be down-sized as a matter of practicality.

Humans simply should not build large population centers in the desert where there is insufficient water to support them for the same reasons that water-intensive crops or livestock/dairy operations should not exist in these water-deprived environments. As an example, over 50 percent of the water in U.S. Colorado River basin ends up being used for the crops and drinking water needs for beef and dairy cattle, not for the humans that depend on this river for their drinking water (Hamilton, 2020). And ironically, most of the beef from these operations is sold in areas such as the Pacific Northwest of the U.S., where water is not nearly as precious as it is in the Southwest U.S. Most of the rest of the water siphoned out of this same basin goes to water-intensive crops and to other desert grown crops that are shipped out of the country as "virtual water" (Borunda, 2020, Pearce, 2006).

A holistic and systems thinking approach to water management and urban planning would not have created these kinds of conditions for cities such as Phoenix, Arizona or Las Vegas, Nevada in the first place. This kind of thoughtful land use planning, in fact, would dramatically alter land and water systems use, ultimately giving a river such as the Colorado River a much greater standing than as simply a body of water to be dammed up and used as desired for commercial farming and livestock enterprises.

Using systems thinking leads to different solutions and often to solutions that seem painfully obvious, after the fact. The vast majority of rivers and streams require no human imposed alterations for either flood protection or transportation and so leaving them alone or removing instream barriers is the simplest and the preferred course of action (Pearce, 2006). When flood control and navigation needs do exist, there are well-founded and well-demonstrated means for meeting these human needs that also allow for the protection and integrity of river ecosystems. Rather than instream dams, for example, a series of low-height instream weirs and pound locks that are less than around three meters high each can be installed if there is the necessity for flood control during the rainy seasons and for river transportation means. These locks have the advantage over dams because they can be intermittently fully opened for fish passage, while allowing silt and sediment to flow downstream without changing the chemistry or temperature of the water downstream. Instream weirs and some lock systems will also need to be fitted with fish ladders, using newer designs that mimic riverbed textures and that are not nearly as high as needed for dams – allowing for upstream and downstream migration, when the locks are needed for extended periods of time. The low height of these weirs and dams protects anadromous smolts or other species from getting nitrogen fixation or temperature shock and the locks allow for much needed sediment and nutrient transport down the river.

Irrigation needs can also be met with existing river systems, either by aquifers recharged by river systems, or with cofferdam stream diversion means placed to the side of a river, all without the need to create lakes formed by instream dams for this use. In other words, irrigation needs for farming can be accomplished without any instream dams at all.

And if hydroelectric power is both warranted and practical in a particular area, then high-head diversion dams using penstocks and powerhouses are a superior alternative to instream dams. These dams are along the side of a river, allowing the river system to flow unimpeded and without artificial instream structures (see Figure 2) below.

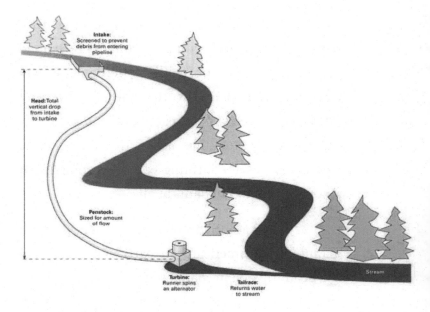

Figure 2 - Note: Anatomy of a high-head, low flow diversion dam hydroelectric site with penstock and powerhouse. GreenBug Energy, (2016).

Design alternatives such as these meet human needs while not significantly or detrimentally altering the natural ecological processes of a given ecosystem. The dam, in fact, is secondary to the river ecosystem as opposed to the river ecosystem being disrupted by the presence of an instream dam. As exemplified here, human interactions with ecosystems need to be well-reasoned, and avoid reductionistic engineering approaches, while also ensuring that the holistic environmental system's needs are prioritized as part of the final solution. In short, this is an example of how the ecosystem's needs are given priority over the human system's needs.

Chapter 8

A Primer on Systems Thinking

Blue mist sits above orange pools in Yellowstone National Park, Wyoming, USA (Amber Leversedge 2015)

Systems thinking is offered now as a new and paradigmatic approach to problem-solving that is perhaps counterintuitive but also certainly a different way of thinking as compared to many past practices. In contrast to reductionist thinking which divides things up and points to precision, this improved way of seeing the world is non-linear and offers a more comprehensive understanding of problems and processes. Systems thinking requires the contemplation of the whole, understand the holistic processes involved with any system and to be aware of the invisible, often counterintuitive processes that are intertwined in any system, human or natural (Wells, 2013).

It has been said that humankind's need for certainty and exactness is like a need for security, "an attempt to flee from the contingency, uncertainty, and the ambivalence of everyday life" (Bernstein, 2005, p. 24). Natural systems, however, appear to satisfy none of these needs and rather are full of uncertainty, complexity and ambiguous outcomes (Benyus, 1997; Wells, 2013). Therefore, an appreciation for and an understanding of the importance of natural systems requires the acceptance of human tendencies toward what may be seen as redundancy and the acceptance of the uncertainty of future outcomes. In the 21st century, new thinking processes aided by a better understanding of needs for natural systems and the need to preserve these systems will greatly help with the grappling of seemingly irreconcilable problems with the help of systems thinking. Clearly, past tendencies to over-simplify problems and to fix problems of our own creation have only made those problems more difficult, thereby putting their solutions further from reach (Senge, 2006; Wells, 2013). Thus, the need now is to learn from the examples of natural systems (Benyus, 1997), and to use these systems as an ally in the fight against the many problems to be faced in the years to come.

There is a direct correlation between systems thinking and arguments made for biomimicry solutions with both schools of thought pointing to Nature for solutions and for a holistic approach to problem solving. Biomimicry makes the case that species, as well as natural systems, have the advantage of millions of years of trial and error solutions. These researchers, such as Benyus (1997), also make the argument that human systems can learn much from natural systems and in ways not yet fully appreciated. Peter Senge

(2006) emphasizes the need to overcome the tendency to think in linear terms and to learn from the many recurrent systems archetypes found in Nature. He warns that human systems are prone to defective structures and offers reminders of the transience of human systems as compared to natural systems. He joins Benyus in making the case that the human species must learn from natural processes if human systems are to be successful over the long run.

Both of these researchers agree with Wells (2013) that systems thinking is needed in order to accept complexity along with a paradigmatic shift that helps one to accept ambiguous outcomes. Both Senge (2006) and Wells (2013) provide the warning that human systems are prone to defectiveness because of human tendencies to ignore the circles of causality found in Nature and due to a lack of awareness of the many recurrent systems archetypes associated with natural systems. These researchers, in turn, are in alignment with those who propose transdisciplinary thinking as opposed to disciplinary thinking. Transdisciplinary researchers warn that single disciplinary thinking again locks one into linear thinking and that this too leads to a lack of awareness of the complexity of systems such as natural systems and again leads to overly simplistic thinking (Montuori, 2005, 2008; Wells, 2013). They also argue that a better understanding of natural systems aids in thinking outside of prevalent disciplinary paradigms allowing a break from well-established patterns of thought and action.

Systems thinkers, biomimicry researchers, and transdisciplinary proponents all see the complexities inherent in natural systems and agree with natural scientists such as botanists, biologists, and ecologists that humankind may never understand enough about any of the Earth's natural systems in order to ever put one back together again after it has been lost. All of these differing researchers from varied disciplines do agree on this one point, it is necessary to preserve that which is not fully understood. In order for one to accept this position, however, requires accepting the complexity and ambiguity of these systems and being comfortable with the realization that complete understanding may never be possible. This kind of systems thinking acceptance affords the ability to accept ambiguity and preservation for preservation's sake.

Perhaps the strongest argument for the revision of the ESA is due to the way many modern scientists think about problem solving now, versus the way most scientists solved problems 50 years ago when the ESA was created. A common misunderstanding of problem solving then and to a lesser extent now is a misconception of where the problem itself truly is. Too often problems have been looked at as simply as possible, as a single piece that can be removed, or altered in a certain way which in turn may correct the issue. In other words, using reductionistic thinking to parse and divide systems in an attempt to increase understanding and facilitate understandable solutions. In contrast, what successful business leaders are learning today, for example, is that rarely is the relationship between a situation and a single entity the best leverage point to enact change. Rather, it is necessary to widen the gaze of how one looks at a situation while also observing the small pieces that make the situation what it is.

Systems are like sentences. They can be simple or complex, but in order to be true to their name, they must contain key structure points. A system must have an input source, a process that achieves something, and an output. For example, an inanimate object is not a system. A stick is not a system. However, inanimate objects can be used as pieces of a system so long as they are achieving something. For example, a tree is a system with a specific purpose - among other things - of growth. A tree is constantly attempting to grow. The inputs into this system are water and sunlight, and the outputs are oxygen, pollen, and leaves - to name just a few. As a view of perspective, a tree is made up of smaller systems, like how it takes in water through its roots, and how it prepares itself for the changing seasons. From another perspective, a single tree is also a small part of a larger system - the forest. And yet, a forest is still a smaller system in what could be a larger system - an ecological zone. With a little imagination, it can become easy to see what size and of what shape a system can be.

There is also a key vernacular that needs to be used when talking about systems. These items are in the glossary and will be talked about in detail when these topics come up. In summary, when thinking about how to identify a system, Donella Meadows refers to four simple questions:

1.) Can the parts be identified?... and

2.) Do the parts affect each other?....and

3.) Do the parts together produce an effect that is different from the effect of each part on its own?... and perhaps

4.) Does the effect, the behavior over time, persist in a variety of circumstances?

(Meadows, p. 13, 2008).

Chapter 9

A Note on System Feedback

River rapids flow through a gorge in Yellowstone National Park, Wyoming USA (Amber Leversedge 2015)

"A feedback loop is formed when changes in a stock affect the flows into or out of that same stock" (Meadows, p. 25, 2008). Feedback loops are important for system analysis for several reasons. A few reasons would be that:

- They can tell us the speed in which iterations within the system happen

- They can tell us if a system has long term sustainability
- They can tell us how stocks affect each other

"When a stock grows by leaps and bounds or declines swiftly or is held within a certain range no matter what else is going on around it, it is likely that there is a control mechanism at work" (Meadows, p. 25, 2008). Not all feedback loops are the same. In fact, sometimes the behavior of feedback loops can dictate how part of a system acts. Sometimes when there are a lot of feedback loops dictating behavior, large parts of the system begin to act in a specific way. "Feedback loops often can operate in two directions... the feedback loop can correct an oversupply as well as undersupply" (Meadows, p. 28, 2008). When a feedback loop has a signaling relationship with a stock, it is called a balancing feedback loop. "Balancing feedback loops are goal-seeking, or stability-seeking" (Meadows, p. 28, 2008).

Reinforcing Feedback loops

One of the powerful effects of systems thinking is the path it can lead down with regard to how one sees not only individual pieces of the world, but also how those pieces may weave themselves into their immediate surroundings and into their further reaching surroundings. Systems thinking provides a level of organizational thought that can help identify causes and effects, as well as identify signals that can spur these actions in the first place. Arguably one of the short-sighted aspects of the ESA is its reductionist thinking, and taking complex pieces of a massive ecosystem and distilling those pieces to singular items on a list, and the key aspects of their environment. Seeing dams as necessary, for example, or only providing passage for fish, ignoring all other species, and then only for fish going upstream across a dam with no thought or consideration that fish also have to travel downstream. This is reductionistic thinking at its finest – well, actually at its worst. With a more comprehensive systems thinking approach, it is more than possible to actually provide better outcomes for these fish species and for all species.

Chapter 10

Current Species Impact - U.S and Worldwide

A geyser basin in Yellowstone National Park, Wyoming, USA
(Amber Leversedge, 2015)

The effects of climate change on the natural world is well documented. Carbon emissions, Greenhouse Gas build-up, and the increased amounts of plastic that are collecting in the world are well-known events that gather much attention in the media. This type of pollution is a collection of negative externalities that have been placed on the natural capital of the planet. One main reason for the existence of these environmental pollutant byproducts lies with systems theory. The direct cost of manufacturing plastic products (labor, raw materials, operations and maintenance, and the cost of energy) are accounted for. However, what is not accounted for are the indirect costs that remain. These are costs like the emissions created from transportation, the cost of the effects of where waste is absorbed back into the environment (plastic doesn't break down easily or quickly). These indirect costs are real, although they are not accounted for on the balance sheets of the producer; nor are they accounted for on the invoice for the consumer. These costs are macro. These costs are produced and fall silently, and at times unnoticed, onto the plates of everyone who breathes oxygen and drinks water. This cost is absorbed by the commons. A collective resource that is used so frequently, that it ironically takes time to stop and consider when one is actually consuming it.

Previously Unrecognized Threats

Humans have always had a complicated history with the natural world. Since the advent of modern humans, however, humankind's ability to mold and impact the world has resulted in noticeable and irreversible changes to the world's ecosystems. Since the expansion of the human species from sub-Saharan Africa, humans have used tools, communication, and complex social structures to become the dominant super-predator on the planet. This trend then advanced the human species into a league of their own as the development of more advanced stages of human existence came to be.

From an economic standpoint, these periods of time can most easily be identified through the observation of technological innovation, the natural advancement of productivity that results. From the Stone Age to the Bronze Age, to the Iron Age, humans have increased their ability to improve their overall quality of life. Using technology to improve their ability to access food, stay safe, and innovate further.

This increased availability of resources naturally set in motion the positive feedback loop that grew life expectancy and advanced the spread of the human species. It wasn't long before civilizations grew and morphed. During this change from ancient to more modern a distinct pattern emerged.

The ability for technological innovation grew at a faster and faster rate, allowing for more and more productivity. Observation of the time it takes to cross to the threshold to the next level of innovation, allows for the observation of a pattern similar to the Golden Spiral (or Golden Ratio) in which the next segment of the curved line is a fraction of the one before it. This is to say that human innovation and growth have accelerated with time, creating more costs and consequences associated with that growth.

By the same token, in order for a system to grow, an input is needed. But, depending on the desired size of the system, there are limits to the amount of input resources available to reach that level of growth. To grow human civilizations, an energy source is needed. Energy systems are no different, however, than most other systems. One key factor is that the output of energy (the waste product that energy production creates) needs to be put somewhere; it needs to be put into some system somewhere.

In a world with a growing economy, that translates into an excess amount of waste energy and that waste energy also translates into an excess of pollution in all forms. From a systems thinking standpoint, therefore, the need for a growing economy becomes of less importance than the need for a thriving environment. In other words, a steady state economy or even a degrowth economy is preferable for the long-term health of environmental systems and ultimately the long-term health of human systems (Beeks, 2016; Jackson, 2009).

Chapter 11

The Anthropocene Epoch

Steam explodes from a geyser in Yellowstone National Park,

Wyoming, USA (Amber Leversedge, 2015)

With the advent of the current growth of human productivity, an incredible amount of pressure has been put on the natural platform that the human species is standing on. The amount of waste in the form of Greenhouse Gas Emissions (GHG) is being collected in the atmosphere in a way that is becoming unsustainable for the system to absorb through its natural means. The human inputs of carbon dioxide, for example, are primarily from ancient pre-historic carbon sinks and are not part of the current carbon cycle. In a system, an inflow will lead to a stock. A stock is a collection point. This can be thought of it like a glass of water being filled at the sink. The volume of the glass dictates the limits to how much water it can hold. Since there is more water available in the pipes leading to the faucet, the water faucet needs to be turned off before the glass of water is overfilled. If the glass of water is overfilled, the overflow will go down the kitchen sink drain - the outflow. A sustainable way to pour a glass of water is to fill the stock to just below the limit of overflow, drink the glass, and if necessary, fill the stock again.

It is in this way that the planet has a way of handling the stock of carbon dioxide and water (two main ingredients in GHG emissions). The ocean and trees absorb a lot of it. Trees need carbon dioxide as part of their photosynthesis process (another system). However, since the level of human productivity - now in its fourth iteration of the industrial revolution - the stock of carbon dioxide is being filled faster than it can be reduced. Side effects of this imbalance of the system result in events like a warming planet, alterations to the ocean currents, extreme weather, and of course species extinction.

There is strong evidence that is linking an unprecedented (and often unseen) amount of species extinction to the negative externalities that have been created by the unprecedented amount of human activity on the planet (Steffen, et al., 2015). The Anthropocene epoch is a geological time period the world is now experiencing. The singular characteristic that differentiates this geological time period from that of any other, is that the measurable amount of planetary changes experienced during this time period are resulting from and correlate directly to the activities of the human species.

Although the Anthropocene epoch began before the passing of the ESA, the authors of this legislation were not likely aware of the extent of these Earth changes to ecosystems or of the extent these changes would be having elsewhere on the planet or consequences in the United States. In addition, discussions about GCC were not common in the 70s and the correlations between GCC and species extinctions are just now being fully appreciated.

Chapter 12

The Connection Between the 6th Great Extinction and the Anthropocene Epoch

Dead pine trees surround an aquamarine hot spring in Yellowstone National Park, Wyoming, USA (Amber Leversedge, 2015)

The 21st century brings with it the severe challenges of an already overpopulated planet, the continued and rampant destruction of natural resources including devastating impacts to ecosystems, and the exhaustion of much needed non-renewable resources (Beeks, 2016). By the middle of the 21st century, humans may experience the complete depletion of the large fish species in the oceans, the exhaustion of most precious and rare earth metals, the end of readily available fossil fuels, a worldwide shortage of clean water, further depletion of already precious lumber resources, and dangerous diminution of available arable land for agriculture, among other catastrophic changes to planet Earth (Millennium Ecosystem Assessment, 2005a, 2005b).

Currently, the Earth is losing ecosystems around the globe at a rate higher than at any time in the last 65 million years and this is what is being called the 6th Great Extinction Event (Klugler, 2014; Macy & Johnstone, 2012; Millennium Ecosystem Assessment, 2005c). The importance of these ecosystems, however, cannot be overstated. According to some research, this loss equates to the end of life on earth, or at least an end to life as it has been known of in the past (Houghton, 1996; Klugler, (2014). This loss of ecosystems equates to loss of distribution and a loss in the numbers of species (see Table 2). In addition to the known benefits of ecosystems such as breathable air, freshwater, essential food, and plentiful renewable resources, there are also countless benefits to the living environment that are not as of yet fully understood. Even so, ecosystems that provide for living systems needs now, and that cannot be duplicated in the future, are vanishing resulting in the loss of essential, albeit, not completely identified benefits forever.

Table 2 - % of species which have lost more than 80% of their distribution between 1900 and 2015

Asia	80 %
Australia	60 %
Africa	55 %
Europe	40 %
N America	> 20 %
S America	~ 20 %

Source – Carrington (2017)

And yet, humanity is aware of the detrimental actions that are leading to climate change, arguably the greatest threat to all species on Earth (Solomon, 2007). Scientists know with little to no uncertainty that human activities are the greatest contributor to ACC, due to deforestation, other land-use changes, fossil fuel consumption, the agricultural industry, livestock practices, the use of toxic refrigerants, and several other practices (Beeks, 2016). The current dilemma has been called the Great Unravelling by Macy and Johnstone (2012). This "is an account, backed by evidence, of the collapse of ecological and social systems, the disturbance of climate, the depletion of resources, and the mass extinction of species" (p. 5).

It is well known and scientifically recognized that atmospheric CO_2, the primary contribution to ACC, are higher now than they have been in 15 million years. This was a time when sea levels were 100 feet higher than they are today and Earth's temperature averages were as much as 10 degrees Fahrenheit higher than now (Tripati, Roberts, & Eagle, 2009). And things are not getting any better for humans or the planet. Earth's atmospheric CO_2 levels rose to 390 ppm in 2009 from 1990 levels of 350 ppm (Jackson, 2009). As of June in 2020, CO_2 levels are well above 415 ppm with an annual steady increase projected for decades to come (CO2Now.org).

The Duality of Human and Natural Systems

There is a popular notion that humans exist on a different level than the natural world. That humans are qualitatively different from the species that share Earth's natural resources. The striking truth is that the closer human understanding is of the behavior of other creatures, the clearer it is that this kind of thinking is both misleading and arrogant. Princeton sociologist Dalton Conley was asked by journalist Steven Dubner to explain what makes humans different from other species. Dalton replied:

> "One by one, the supposed attributes that we had thought were unique to humans have been shown to be present in other species: Crows use tools; elephants can recognize themselves in a mirror; whales form social networks of the same size and complexity as we do; penguins mourn their dead; gibbons are monogamous; bonobos are polyamorous; ducks rape; chimpanzees deploy slaves; velvet spiders commit

suicide; dolphins have language. And the quicker we get over the Judeo-Christian notion that we are somehow qualitatively different from the rest of the biome, the quicker we will learn to live healthier lives for ourselves and for the planet."

With that logic in mind, it would make sense that since humans cannot escape from the systemic relationship with other species, and since humans share so many social similarities with these other species, then humans should observe the natural systems in place and gain guidance through the problem-solving process of how the whole of the systems can be protected, rather than making a checklist of individual species and their directly associated habitats.

The following checklist is applicable here, as it pertains to how problem solvers can adjust their thinking away from ESA reductionistic thinking to systems thinking when addressing the pressing problems of species and ecosystems loss:

- End the improper emphasis on just the species as a part of an ecosystem. Rather an emphasis needs to be placed on the whole of the ecosystem with the species itself as a single stock within that system.

- A single stock being eliminated is a small piece of the problem. There may still be other stocks that might be low (endangered) and still other stocks that are overflowing.

- It is necessary to understand the wider scope of protection (especially with the combined efforts of the clean air and water acts); albeit still missing much of the issues - that all of these points are interconnected within the system itself.

- Metrics are useful, they measure change and progress, but the reductionistic process of checking off a box is analogous to sticking one's finger in the dike and thinking the problem is solved.

- The ESA is working, over 40 species have recovered. But what about the Anthropocene era, the insect apocalypse, the 6th great extinction event, and what is the difference between checkboxes and small specific victories?

- What is needed is a holistic approach, which could use the same amount of resources, but has wider-reaching positive effects?

Chapter 13

Justice and Ecosystem Protection

A view of a lake in Glacier National Park, Montana, USA
(Amber Leversedge, 2015)

Although the popular forms of justice – recognition, distributive, and participatory are often discussed in terms of human social justice, their principles can also be applied to natural ecosystems. A greater understanding of how these ideas interact with each other can improve the likelihood of ethical ecosystem management and protection. For example, the idea of recognition justice is particularly important to indigenous peoples given their history of cultural connection to natural ecosystems and their deeply embedded knowledge of "environmental harm that may not normally be considered" (White 2014, pg. 44) by those further removed from the system.

Recognition justice is also vital to ecosystem protection and the rights of indigenous peoples as a "corrective action" that can begin to repair past environmental and cultural damage at the hands of settlers and colonialism forces (Aragao, Jacobs, & Cliquet, 2016, pg. 223). These same concepts can be applied even when indigenous populations do not inhabit an ecosystem, through the recognition of the needs of non-human species. Just as the rights of indigenous peoples must be recognized so too must the rights of ecosystems be recognized as predating the laws of the current legal systems.

As with recognition justice, the principles of distributive justice apply to ecosystem protection in much the same way that they apply to other social systems – through the examination of benefits and burdens. The idea of burdensome scenarios applies to non-human animals who are often the first to experience the fallout of damaging anthropogenic activity.

Biodiversity loss as a result of land degradation, for example, is one of the many wicked problems facing the globe, and while some humans may be reaping the benefits of this land degradation, non-humans are experiencing the greatest burdens.

Distributive justice for an ecosystem would mean the assurance of "equal access to the benefits of ecosystem services," (Aragao, Jacobs, & Cliquet, 2016, pg. 222), and not just for humans. Distributive justice is also integral to the consideration of intergenerational justice (Aragao, Jacobs, & Cliquet, 2016), which is a critical incentive for ecosystem protection.

Ethical ecosystem management serves to benefit not only current generations of human and non-human creatures but to also ensure that future generations of animals and people will be able to experience the benefits of a healthy and productive ecosystem.

Participatory or procedural justice is concerned with the "legitimation of decision-making procedures," (Aragao, Jacobs, & Cliquet, pg. 222) and necessitates the inclusion of diverse groups when making political and social decisions. This process applies to ecosystem protection when the needs of non-human animals and plants – and by extension, their holistic ecosystem – are considered when making political decisions. Importantly, this approach must also include the views of indigenous tribes in the convening process for reasons previously mentioned. Participatory justice remains critical to successful ecosystem protection in order to ensure that political motivations do not outweigh considerations of the natural environment, as has often been the case throughout human history. While this is an ongoing battle, further discussions of how to speak for natural entities in a political and legal realm can improve this process and lead to better representation for these entities in the public sphere.

Chapter 14

Conceptualizing the Rights of Nature

Dense forest surrounds a lake in Boulder, Colorado with the snow-capped Rocky Mountains in the distance (Louise Campbell, 2017)

The Rights of Nature (RoN) approach advocates for the recognition of natural entities as beings with rights worthy of protection, just as humans are afforded basic rights. In fact, Schlosberg writes, "The recognition of nature is the pretext, or the context, necessary for a better distribution of environmental goods and bads...in this sense, extending recognition to nature is not unlike extending recognition with regard to issues of gender, culture, or sexuality" (2001, p. 13).

It is argued here as well that this new legal recognition of Nature's rights requires a systems thinking approach to problem solving combined with a holistic understanding of how natural systems function.

RoN is a new ecological governance that is considered by many as the most effective tool to allow ecosystems to flourish independent of human interference and placing Nature's needs before human needs. By giving natural systems personhood status, this requires that human needs must align and be configured within the limits of Nature rather than the other way around (see Figure 3). This legal status change for natural systems has become necessary not only because of continued degradation of natural systems, but because laws around the world apply almost exclusively to humans, leaving natural systems and other species out of the arguments for justice. The legal arguments supporting this paradigm shift are that current law structures are based on outdated 17th century thinking that were mechanistic, adversarial and anthropocentric (Ito, 2017). From that time to the present, natural systems and resources have been seen as ways to gain capital, and as such ecosystems have been monetized for their resource potential.

RoN, however, gives Nature the highest hierarchy of rights because all life depends on it followed by human rights and lastly with corporate rights (often negative) being given the lowest rights in this hierarchy (see Figure 3). It is noteworthy that with this RoN circular image to the right, that the only circle that can exist on its own is the Nature circle.

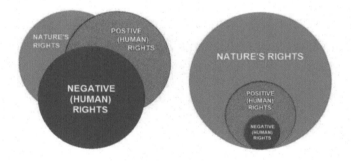

Figure 3 – Note: Nestled Rights: The needed paradigm shift to the right nestled rights in order to ensure RoN to natural systems. Halstead (n.d.)

While RoN has been an important step in the goal of more ethical environmental protection, some argue that in practice RoN can legitimize environmental degradation within certain predetermined limits (Community Environmental

Legal Defense Fund, 2016). For example, pollution of waterways is typically tolerated as long as certain thresholds are not surpassed – from a holistic ecosystem justice perspective, this does not provide ecosystem protection, but rather it may ensure that pollution can continue without retribution. This can further devalue ecosystems and perpetuate the narrative that Nature exists to fulfill anthropogenic needs and desires, further separating humans from the natural system of which they are a critical component.

Despite this potential shortcoming, RoN has allowed for further dialogue of what humans owe to natural ecosystems – not just from the perspective of anthropogenic needs but also based on their intrinsic value. One of the functions of RoN is to legally consider "landscapes...as entities possessing jurisdictional rights akin to those of corporations" (Gordon, 2018, pg. 50). In fact, the likening of natural entities to corporations has allowed for the further justification of RoN, based on past legislative decisions that have afforded companies with similar legal rights (Gordon, 2018).

RoN has also been particularly integral to the belief system of many indigenous tribes, based on their view that human wellbeing is "intertwined with the welfare of all earth ecosystems" and that human activities must, therefore, be "based on ecological foundations" (Kaufman & Martin, 2017, pg. 132).

Attaching a legal status to natural entities in this manner can prescribe more power to the natural world and be a crucial pathway for full ecosystem protection, partly because laws have the ability to "articulate a broad range of values" that may not be otherwise considered in "individualistic and economic valuation methods" (Aragao, Jacobs, & Cliquet, 2016, pg. 132). As with any movement to secure rights, there are challenges associated with a RoN framework, namely in the broad understanding of the term and the different ways it can be interpreted as a result. The following section will discuss varying forms of implementation for a RoN framework, each with its own challenges and successes.

Chapter 15

Rights of Nature in Action

A secluded cove near Monterey, California, USA (Louise

Campbell, 2017)

In the past decade, the principles of RoN have taken hold across the globe. Some of the locations where RoN efforts have taken place include United States municipalities, New Zealand, India, and Ecuador, among others. (Kauffman & Martin, 2017). The idea has also gained popularity at a number of global climate conferences and features in numerous agreements aimed at combating global climate change and land degradation (Kauffman & Martin, 2017). Many of these instances require the participation of a "human manager," or group which is willing to continuously advocate on the behalf of RoN even if it has been declared a national principle, due to the state's unique positionality to both "exploit *and* protect" the environment based on political motivations and case-by-case challenges (Kincaid, 2019, pg. 563).

Varying levels of success have been seen in almost every state that has adopted a RoN framework – a comprehensive understanding of the challenges and successes of each of these attempts can better inform future efforts to ensure ethical ecosystem protection through the use of RoN.

As the first nation to recognize the rights of natural entities in its constitution, Ecuador has had a widespread influence on the concept of RoN in other countries. The Ecuadorian constitution proclaims Nature as an entity with the right "'to exist, persist, maintain, and regenerate its vital cycles'" (Ecuadorian Constitution, 2008, qtd. in Gordon, 2018, pg. 52). The wording of this phrase is worth noting for its exclusion of any human motivations, suggesting that Nature has this right inherently and not solely to further anthropogenic needs.

It has also been argued, based on the legal decisions made in favor of corporations and extractive activities since the RoN framework's inception, that the Ecuadorian government was motivated by a need to "justify and legitimize its development agenda" (Kauffman & Martin, 2017, pg. 131) and that RoN legislation has been used as a shield for doing so. Nonetheless, this country's efforts have still been favorably acknowledged in the global environmental community and many view Ecuador's efforts as an important step towards more ethical ecosystem protection, despite the occasional abuse of the laws.

New Zealand's conceptualization of RoN has been recognized as a more applied understanding of ecosystem rights that may have the ability to truly impact environmental protection. In March of 2017, parliament "passed legislation declaring Te Awa Tupua – the river and all its physical and metaphysical elements – an indivisible, living whole" (Warne, 2019, para. 7).

The positive reception of this declaration is based on the inclusion of the indigenous Maori tribe in the process to declare RoN for a number of sacred ecosystems – not only were principles of recognition and participatory justice met, but the New Zealand government was aware of the need for a more holistic approach to addressing the environmental degradation of these sites, which ultimately included "820 square miles of forests, lakes, and rivers" (Warne, 2019, para. 8). This has been considered a success not only for the people and government of New Zealand, who view these steps as addressing a "long-standing injustice" (Warne, 2019, para. 12) on the part of settlers and polluting practices but also for the Maori Tribe and their consistent advocacy for the natural world. For the tribe, the mention of legality is less important than the changing conversations about ecosystem protection which support "a new orientation of humans to the natural world," focused "not [only] on rights but responsibilities" (Warne, 2019, para. 11).

Legal analysts have further applauded the New Zealand rights declaration for its focus on the intrinsic value of natural systems and "rejection of a human-centered rights regime for protecting Nature as property" (Gordon, 2018, pg. 52). Coming almost a decade after the Ecuadorian constitutional provision for RoN, the New Zealand declaration presents a promising case for further progress in holistic ecosystem protection based on value-focused narratives, indigenous recognition, and more inclusive participation.

Where Rights of Nature are Absent

While the idea of RoN has been gaining global traction, there are still many countries where the idea of declaring natural ecosystems as possessing intrinsic rights to be in direct conflict to their state-supported actions. This is particularly prevalent in Malaysia and Indonesia via the divisive, devastating and ecosystems degrading process of palm oil harvesting. Palm oil is a pervasive substance used in the manufacturing of thousands of processed foods, and these two countries have become a hub for production. While these processes have contributed greatly to the economic development of these nations (Pye, 2019), its production places heavy burdens on ecosystems.

The destructive production of palm oil has led to "continued crises of biodiversity loss and forest fires," as well as increases in soil subsidence, flooding, and pollution (Pye, 2019, pg. 218). These problems have only worsened in recent years, given that palm oil "now accounts for a staggering 70% of agricultural land use" (Pye, 2019, pg. 218) in these countries.

The palm oil industry in Malaysia and Indonesia exemplifies the distributive, recognition, and participatory injustices that can occur when the intrinsic values of Nature are not recognized and declared. Any hope for the provision of such rights for the threatened land and species inhabiting these lands in these areas is weakened by the industry's close ties to state motivations (Pye, 2019), making the operation "highly concentrated and politically organized" (Pye, 2019, pg. 219).

While attempts have been made to ensure sustainable practices, environmentally degrading practices are in some ways unavoidable through the production of this resource, which has led to false declarations of environmental stewardship and the "commodification of sustainability" (Pye, 2019, pg. 221) on behalf of the industries in question.

If a RoN framework were to be adopted and truly honored in these countries, it would be more difficult for corporations operating in the area to justify their actions in the quest for palm oil, and the result would likely be widespread protection of threatened ecosystems and the diverse species that live and migrate through these areas.

Chapter 16

Creating a Future of Ecosystems Justice

A coastal view, taken near Monterey, California, USA (Louise Campbell, 2017)

For decades, environmentalists have advocated for a comprehensive understanding of Nature as valuable beyond human uses and deserving of rights and recognition as a result. In the famed Sand County Almanac, Aldo Leopold stated that "in wildness is the salvation of the world" (1949, pg. 133), an idea that is continuing to

144

gain traction as more and more natural ecosystems are threatened by anthropogenic climate change and other human-centric actions. Leopold called for a "land ethic" as an extension to commonly-held community ethics, which he argued simply "enlarges the boundaries...to include soil, waters, plants, and animals, or collectively: the land" (1949, pg. 204).

These ideas were later built upon by scholars Paul W. Taylor and Peter Singer, who further advocated for the rights of animals and wild places. Taylor encouraged the perception of plants and animals as "entities with inherent worth" that humans "are morally bound to protect or promote" the wellbeing of, not for the humans' sake, but "for *their* sake" (1981, pg. 198). Similarly, Singer argued that rights must be "extended to other species" based on the "basic principle of equality" and the idea that "if a being suffers, there can be no moral justification for refusing to take that suffering into consideration" (1989, n.p.). The actualization of these arguments, while limited, provides an important framework for the consideration of intrinsic value within natural systems.

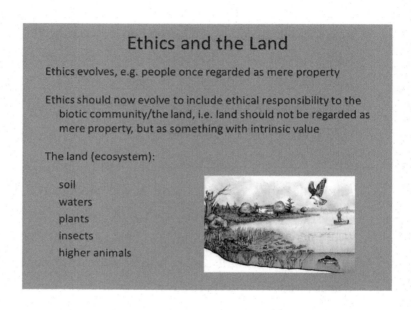

Figure 4 – Note: A Leopold pictorial pointing to ethical responsibilities to Land, the land community and the intrinsic value of land. (Slideplayer, n.d.)

Aldo Leopold's proclamation that land has life needs to be taken both figuratively and literally (see Figure 4). Most conservationists today see that an ecosystem has a figurative life of its own because it is self-sustaining and comprised of so many interacting players that have dependencies on the whole of the system. But there is also the literal life that exists both on the macroscopic scale and the microscopic scale. Humans see most of the macroscopic life and the interactions that take place between many of these animal and plant species. Just as importantly, however, there is a vast amount of microscopic life in both land and water ecosystems that most humans do not consider because it is out of view. As discussed previously, organic soil contains more than one million microorganisms in each gram of soil (Mass, 2016). It is these microorganisms as well as the vastly complex soil chemistry of each land ecosystem that defines what kind of an ecosystem exists in any particular place and what kinds of macroscopic life can exist within these well-established conditions.

The same holds true for water systems, with as many as a half million zooplankton being found in just one-gallon of sea water (Chesapeake Bay Program, 2020). These microorganisms in water systems such as both zooplankton and phytoplankton have just as profound an influence on the life forms found within water systems as compared with the fungus, bacteria, algae and actinomycetes, etc. found in land systems. Both of these systems have so much life within them, that it can be said that these ecosystems are living entities, even though humans may not see the underlying life that supports them and that makes each of them unique.

This literal description of life in ecosystems then supports Leopold's position that land has life, augmented here to state that water has life as well. Accepting either the figurative or the intrinsic life associations with either land or water ecosystems leads to the acceptance of the need for the protection of these living systems.

It is argued here, therefore, that both land-based ecosystems and water-based ecosystems are living entities in and of themselves.

To get to the specifics of how RoN designations can be implemented successfully around the world, two justice and sustainability scholars at Arizona State University were interviewed about their beliefs on the topic and ecosystem protection more generally, and certain similarities in ideas stand out as possible areas for future intervention in environmental protection. Joan McGregor, a Professor in the School of Philosophy, Historical, and Religious Studies, was particularly concerned with the interrelation of ecosystem protection and intergenerational justice – for her, RoN is a question of "inheritance," based on the idea that future people deserve the right to make their own decisions regarding the natural environment; further degradation of fragile ecosystems could prevent that right from existing (personal communication, November 5, 2019). She further argued that ecosystems can be valued in a number of ways, including spiritual, recreational, aesthetic, and economic terms (McGregor, personal communication, November 5, 2019). While this conceptualization of the values of ecosystems does not take into account intrinsic values, it is important to recognize that "pragmatically, talking about interspecies justice in terms of human benefit often leads to greater action" (McGregor, personal communication, November 5, 2019). While intrinsic valuations of Nature are important and ultimately necessary to holistic protection, it can also be extremely beneficial to recognize that humans play a powerful role in determining how ecosystems are protected and that therefore framing priorities based on anthropocentric needs is not always a condemnable action. This sort of framing can also encourage a greater understanding of the interconnections between humans and their non-human counterparts, which can lead to an increased sense of responsibility.

Christopher Boone, Dean of the School of Sustainability at Arizona State University, argued that part of the solution towards ecosystem protection must be based on elevating discussions surrounding environmental ethics (personal communication, November 21, 2019). He called for a reconceptualization of how one thinks about conservation – noting that most scholars say there is no "wilderness" left, or no parcel of the land untouched by humans, Boone argued that a failure to integrate humans into ecosystem management could ultimately lead to unsuccessful attempts at ecosystem protection (personal communication, November 21, 2019). This also relates to participatory justice and the idea that people who know the land have to be included in the discussion. Boone further noted the importance of rejecting a false dichotomy in which certain entities have to be prioritized over others, as this can create further conflict in places where compromise could be the better option (personal communication, November 21, 2019). Importantly, Boone is also a strong advocate for a holistic systems-thinking approach when addressing complex challenges such as ecosystem protection. While Boone, like McGregor, was more concerned with the role of humans in ecosystem protection, his perspective on the issue further exemplifies the diverse ways that the challenge can be approached based on the needs of the situation.

Seventy years ago, Leopold argued that the "extension of ethics" to ecology was "an evolutionary possibility and an ecological necessity" (1949, pg. 203). Now, in the 21st century, with the threats of global climate change, land degradation, and mass extinction becoming quite visible, these ideas are even more essential. Leopold recognized, during what is often lauded as the "golden age" of America, that civilization would be faced with the choice between a "higher standard of living" and "things natural, wild, and free" (1949, pg. vii). This choice has been made again and again since he made this observation, and until recently human progress was almost always prioritized. The implementation of the Rights of Nature and holistic ecosystem protection in places such as New Zealand have begun to shift the discourse from what value Nature has for humans to what value Nature has in and of itself. Through more widespread adoption of these principles, humans have the ability to correct for past injustices against indigenous communities, plants and non-human animals, and entire natural systems.

Policy Changes Needed

Policy Changes Needed - United States and Other Nations

Federal policies will without a doubt be a crucial role in guaranteeing certain rights of Nature. This can be done in several ways but success in countries such as the United States would likely be found within ecosystems protection legislation, something that will protect a species and its environment without detrimentally impacting economic potential in a given country.

There is often a fear, for example within the United States, that environmental protection policy comes with strings of job loss and other economic inhibitors. Conceptually, capitalism will still be able to exist under ecosystem protection laws.

The United States has experimented with both market-based and regulatory policies in the past to encourage behavioral shifts within industry, one of the most famous examples being the cap-and-trade program. But, "too much regulatory policy can quickly get out of hand...stifle innovativeness as well as production" (Beeks & Ziko, 2018).

However, market-based policies alone do not encourage environmental protection and may further alienate both industry and consumers from environmental awareness. Environmental protection policies from the past have tried to distinguish between human and natural roles, but one simply cannot function without the other and so policy needs to reflect this reality. Sean Kelly explains it best in his second of five principles of integral ecology, "The core insight of ecology, however, is that no system including individual ecosystems, can be isolated from (eco)systems in which it is embedded...a central task of a more integral Gaia theory will be to illuminate the complex relationship between the human and the rest of the planetary ecosphere" (Mickey, Kelly, & Robbert, 2017).

Effective legislation in countries such as the United States will account for both human and natural roles, and recognize the ecosystem as vital to both organism and environment. And this legislation must also account for the need for connectivity conservation between ecosystems and provide for the protection of interacting ecosystems that in many cases cross national borders.

In these cases, international protection is needed in addition to national regulations for ecosystem protection (Krosby, et al., 2015).

These kinds of legislated protections are what living environments need and this is precisely what the well-intentioned ESA has failed to do, it has failed to protect the full ecosystem in which the species they aim to protect relies on. Take for example the case of the Marbled Murrelet a "threatened" bird species under the ESA, these sea-going birds rely on old-growth (more than 80 years old), dense, multi-layered coastal forests in the Northwest U.S. that cannot be fragmented. These forests have fallen victim to commercial timber harvesting and other destructive practices such as human-induced fires which have caused a declining Marbled Murrelet population (USFWS, 2020).

Logging operations on both private and federal land break up the old-growth forests that this species and hundreds of others depend up, with a decline in this species alone of 30% since 1992 (USFWS, 2020).

Declines such as this could have been prevented with a more encompassing piece of legislation, to protect not just the species, but the entire ecosystem. Alternatively, a regional-scale "ecosystem protection" legislation was introduced in the Senate back in 2016, known as the Northern Rockies Ecosystem Protection Act (NREPA). Under NREPA, 23 million acres of land would be protected as it would be considered a land vital to ecosystems and watersheds (Tamaqua Borough Sewage Sludge Ordinance, 2006). NREPA was designed to cater towards the American public by ensuring such environmental protection would not pose any sort of economic threat by stating, "[the act] provides opportunities for employment in outdoor trades by establishing rehabilitation zones on specific tracts of damaged Federal land where active restoration work will occur; provide a contract for local business and will renew the intrinsic economic, social, and cultural benefits that result from productive land" (Tamaqua Borough Sewage Sludge Ordinance, 2006).

On a national scale, similar legislation should be proposed in which the ESA could be supplemented with an Endangered Ecosystems Act (or the equivalent). This legislation needs to take into account the Rights of Nature practices both in the United States and in other countries to protect important ecosystems from human-induced degradation. Language from RoN laws around the world will need to be incorporated into this new ecosystem's protection legislation. This legislation will also need to include language stating that a critical benefit of protecting ecosystems is the added benefit provided to human communities with Nature provided services such as cleaner water and cleaner air being shared with those human communities.

Therefore, a proposed legislation that may be called an Endangered Ecosystems Act can be further strengthened by including a "Rights of Nature" component. In 2006, Schuylkill County, Pennsylvania forged the way for similar legislation when they passed the Tamaqua Borough Sewage Sludge Ordinance, "to protect the health, safety, and welfare of the residents of Tamaqua Borough, the soil, groundwater, and surface water, the environment, and its flora and fauna, and the practice of sustainable agriculture, the Borough finds it necessary to ban corporations and other limited liability entities from engaging in the land application of sewage sludge" (Tamaqua Borough Sewage Sludge Ordinance, 2006). With this RoN legislation, Schuylkill County took an unprecedented step to grant the Borough ecosystem the same rights of a "person" while at the same time revoking personhood rights from corporations, "Borough residents, natural communities, and ecosystems shall be considered to be 'persons' for purposes of the enforcement of the civil rights of those residents, natural communities, and ecosystems...corporations engaged in land application of sludge...shall not be 'persons' under the United States or Pennsylvania Constitutions" (Tamaqua Borough Sewage Sludge Ordinance, 2006).

In its unprecedented move to grant an entire ecosystem legal protection, Tamaqua Borough became one of the first places in the world to adopt RoN policies.

Many will protest the idea of granting rights to Nature, but as law Professor Christopher Stone points out, "each time there is a movement to confer rights onto some new 'entity,' the proposal is bound to sound odd or frightening or laughable. This is partly because until the rightless thing receives its rights, it cannot be seen as anything but a thing for the use of 'us' - those who are holding rights at the time" (Stone, 1972, p. 455). American history is littered with generation-defining moments when basic rights were granted to groups that at one point had seemed ridiculous like women being granted the right to vote or establishing that the same basic rights apply to black men as they do white men just to name a few!

An Endangered Ecosystems Act is one of the most effective ways to address the current gaps in American environmental policy. This proposed Endangered Ecosystems Act must, however, include RoN language. Using the ESA, NREPA, and the Tamaqua Borough case as examples will provide an excellent road map for how such a policy would play out on a national scale. The U.S. is quickly losing biodiversity due in part to the tendency to separate the species from the environment, just "60% of 261 major terrestrial ecosystems in the United States and Puerto Rico, defined by the Bailey-Kuchler classification, were represented in designated wilderness areas in 1988" (Noss, LaRoe, & Scott, n.d.).

Part of the problem is that many of the federal agencies tasked with monitoring the environment do not include nationwide ecosystem monitoring. Noss, et. al. assert the EPA does not monitor the statuses of "specific vegetation types of habitats in a manner useful for our purposes." The need is there for this kind of monitoring and active management for the restoration of critical plant species as needed to restore certain ecosystems.

The proposed Endangered Ecosystems Act will include provisions to task the EPA with measuring levels of ecosystem endangerment. As with the ESA, any ecosystem found to be critically endangered will be given protections that prevent further destruction. Under the ESA there is a provision to require habitat protections, known as critical habitat areas," but this could be greatly strengthened with the addition of an Endangered Ecosystems Act in which RoN could be granted. Meaning using RoN in the Endangered Ecosystems Act would ensure the protection of the endangered species by doing what Tamaqua Borough did in Pennsylvania. The timber logging companies that infiltrate the old-growth forests, for example, that endangered species rely upon would be denied personhood rights, and instead, these rights would be granted to the ecosystem as a whole, making it illegal to disrupt or destroy the ecosystem.

RoN protection can shield endangered ecoystems such as temperate grasslands, in which over 98% have been degraded by human actions (Marris, 2020). With systems such as these restored, endangered keystone species such as the prairie dog can be returned, with only 2% of this species still surviving today due primarily to the loss of 95% of their natural habitats and due to human-introduced diseases. Their habitat loss includes the vast majority of the Great Plains in the U.S., for example, having been turned into farmland and pastureland (Wade, 2020).

As societies learn to remove meat from their diets and as they move away from many commercial farming practices, perhaps, as much as 50% of historic temperate grasslands, now used as farmlands, can be restored and protected under RoN laws (Hawken, 2017; Oppenlander, 2013; Wade, 2020). Habitats such as these can be returned to the historic inhabitants of prairie dog ecosystems such as black-tailed prairie dogs, burrowing owls, coyote, black-footed ferrets, bison, swift foxes, pronghorn sheep, golden eagles, snakes, cottontail rabbits, jackrabbits, the greater sage grouse, the mountain plover, wolves, beavers, grasshopper mouse, the deer mouse, horned lark, the mountain plover, ferruginous hawk, bobcats, toads, narrow-mouthed frogs and salamanders, just to name a few (Predator Conservation Alliance, 2001).

And perhaps just as importantly – greatly diminished grassland species such as switch grass or big bluestem grasses, purple prairie coneflower, sagebrush and the shorter buffalo grass that were common in much of the plains in the U.S. can be returned to these grasslands. It is known now that the heavy, deep roots of many plains grasses that have been replaced by farm crops and cattle grazing pastures had been Nature's way of sequestering carbon, a critical function that has been lost with present-day commercial agriculture and livestock operations (Hawken, 2017). Returning these temperate grasslands to their natural state, in fact, is one of the greatest strategies humans can use to drawdown CO_2 from the atmosphere (Hawken, 2017).

Policy Changes Needed - International

Intergovernmental bodies such as the United Nations will play an instrumental part in crafting trans-border statutes to recognize the rights of Nature. The United Nations should be encouraged to formally adopt a Declaration on the Rights of Nature. This has previously been suggested at the 2010 World People's Conference on Climate Change and the Rights of Mother Earth where they concluded, "affirming that to guarantee human rights it is necessary to recognize and defend the rights of Mother Earth and all beings in her and that there are existing cultures, practices, and laws to do so" (Global Alliance for the Rights of Nature, 2019).

The United Nations 2015 Sustainable Development Goals (SDG) provide the perfect framework to incorporate RoN as it fosters many of the same ideals the UN already seeks to advance. A formal Declaration on the Rights of Nature would recognize the inherent rights Nature has which include: the right to exist, the right to be respected, the right to water, the right to clean air, and the right to integral health among other things (Global Alliance for the Rights of Nature, 2019).

The 2013, "Stillheart Declaration" which was formed by a group of 32 global social movement leaders which and included indigenous leaders, economists, ecologists, and other climate advocates provides an already globalized framework which declares that the current rule of law placing human needs over that of Nature must be changed, "Rights of Nature or Rights of Mother Earth seek to define equal legal rights for ecosystems to 'exist, flourish, and regenerate their natural capacities'...transform our human relationship with Nature from property-based to legal rights-bearing entity" (Global Exchange, 2017).

A UN declaration could create international precedents to declare Rights of Nature as the law of the land. Following the framework provided by "The Stillheart Declaration" and the framework written by the members of the 2010 World People's Conference on Climate Change, a formal UN Declaration on the Rights of Nature should include the following statements as outlined in "The Stillheart Declaration":

- Laws of Nature supersede rights to property
- There should be no separation between how Nature is treated and how humans are treated
- Nature is the foundation of life itself
- Reject market-based mechanisms that allow the quantification and commodification of Earth's natural process, rebranded as 'ecosystem services'
- Indigenous people must be empowered by legal and cultural norms as partners or caretakers of the land and territories in which they live (Global Exchange, 2017).

The SDGs first began taking form over two decades before their publication at the United

Nations Conference on Environment and Development in Rio de Janeiro, Brazil in June of 1992. Here, Agenda 21 was drafted and became one of the first comprehensive and truly actionable plans for sustainable international development. Chapter 8, Section 8.13-8.22 of Agenda 21 makes for a good outline that describes how the UN could provide support to member-states under the Declaration on the Rights of Nature. For example, Section 8.16 states:

"To support countries that request it in their national efforts to modernize and strengthen policy and legal framework of governance for sustainable development....To encourage the development and implementation of national, state, provincial, and local programs that assess and promote compliance and respond appropriately to non-compliance" (United Nations Division for Sustainable Development, 1992).

One of the main functions of the UN in regards to global RoN policy would be to oversee and assist member states as they incorporate the new international standards they are called upon to adopt under the Declaration on the Rights of

Nature. In other words, the UN would be responsible for ensuring member states pass RoN legislation through their respective national governing bodies, this would also ensure a sense of sovereignty among member states by which RoN legislation could be drafted to accordingly fit their respective countries individualized needs while still complying to the UN Declaration. Another reason it is vital the UN plays such an overarching role over international RoN policy is for handling disputes when ecosystem protection involves a transborder disagreement.

Ecosystems, of course, are not bound by borders, and so there will be many cases where ecosystem protection will cross national borders. To manage such discrepancies, the United Nations will thus be granted jurisdiction over transboundary ecosystem protection disputes.

The World Trade Organization (WTO) could also help in international disputes as well as implement market-based approaches to ecosystem conservation. It has also been proposed that a UN World Environmental Organization (WEO) could be formulated to enforce appropriate policies and take actions such as trade sanctions for the benefit of environmental systems (Beeks & Ziko, 2018).

This could be most helpful, for example, when discussing ways to mitigate the effects of deforestation in the Amazon Rainforest, "A WEO could enforce eco-taxes for the use of virgin or old-growth timber and by doing so, protect ecosystems by making their resources more costly than timber farm lumber" (Beeks & Ziko, 2018, p. 16).

The cyclical irony about the state of the Amazon Tropical Forest is a great example for helping one to understand why an international Declaration on the Rights of Nature is so important. It is clear today that Brazilian policy entertains the idea of expanding agricultural land even at the expense of rainforest protections. But Brazil's eagerness to increase agricultural production is arguably a result of global demand for production rather than higher production leading to greater demand. And given the destruction caused by this higher production, western countries chastise Brazil's treatment of the

Amazon Rainforest and its indigenous inhabitants, despite doing the same to their own lands centuries earlier *and* being the reason for the high demand for products made under conditions of massive deforestation.

The leaders who crafted "The Stillheart Declaration" recognized this hypocrisy and understood that sure, part of the issue was a blasé attitude towards environmental destruction, but more than that it is the great flaw in the globalized economy which consistently seeks profit, profit, and profit.... An international Declaration on the Rights of Nature presents itself as a potential turning point in the world's future. Only through global recognition of Nature's intrinsic value, not for the sake of profit but for the sake of living, can the hope to see the living environment and ecosystems protected as living entities be realized.

Chapter 17

Promise for the Future

A lone boat makes its way across the San Francisco Bay,

California, USA (Louise Campbell, 2017)

As of 2020, as much as 50% of the land

space on Earth has had minimal impact from

humans. And as of 2020, there are bold calls to set aside all of that 50% by 2050 for Nature and to keep any human interaction to a contained level from that point on (Kerlin, 2020). This crucial discussion will continue at the next meeting of the Convention on Biological Diversity in 2021. The current ideas are not to set aside all of these areas as parks or as Wilderness areas, but to have them managed and cared for with many of the suggestions in this paper being considered. RoN considerations are being discussed along with ideas ranging from nature friendly agricultural projects all the way to strict land use protection that excludes much of any human interaction and a host of ideas between these two extremes.

Unfortunately, the 50% that has been heavily impacted is not a well-balanced distribution of human use, with some ecosystems such as temperate grasslands, tropical coniferous forests and tropical dry forests all having over 99% heavy impacts (Marris, 2020).

Therefore, strong consideration needs to be given to restoration of ecosystems such as these by first taking them out of human hands and then restoring them through active management to return them to their natural state.

 And high priority must be given to those ecosystems that have the greatest diversity of species living in them in order to protect the largest numbers of species – both plants and animals. Great consideration needs to also be given to those areas under the most threat such as the East China Sea, Indonesia, India and Northern Europe (Marris, 2020).

There is much to discuss, but the great promise for all is that these discussions for these kinds of options are ongoing concerning needs other than just human needs, with the kind of urgency required to enact change for the benefit of other species. And these talks do need to consider the legal protection benefits of RoN designations across the board, from the very small to the very large ecosystems. These talks also need to consider all of the world's water ecosystems as well, as they are under at least as much threat as are land systems. There is every reason to suggest, in fact, that RoN designations be enacted on a grand scale for the sake of not just the land and water systems that are less impacted, but on vast areas of land and water that are overused today.

Here's to RoN designations for the Entire Amazon Forest, all of the world's tropical forests, the Amazon River, the Columbia and Nile Rivers, all of the world's great rivers, the Entire Great Barrier Reef, and all of the world's coral reefs, all of the world's uninhabited islands, the Boreal Forests all across the planet, all of Antarctica, the Arctic sea and the Arctic icecaps, the Arctic tundra all across the planet, the entire Kalahari desert, the Sahara desert, all of the world's coastal wetlands and the entire Tibetan Plateau, all of the world's great mountain ranges, and these are only a beginning list of areas of the world needing RoN protection. 50% protection of the Earth's land is a great goal to start off with but it does not have to end there. The ecosystems in these places and many other places have just as much right to life as any human being does and it is past time that human systems of justice are used to grant them these rights.

References

Andersen, M. S. (2007). An introductory note on the environmental economics of the circular economy. *Sustainability Science, 2*(1), 133–140.

Aragao, Alexandra; Jacobs, Sander; Cliquet, An. (2016). "What's law got to do with it? Why environmental justice is essential to ecosystem service valuation." *Ecosystem Services*, vol. 22, ph. 221-227.

ASU. (n.d.). Plants of the temperate forest. Retrieved from https://askabiologist.asu.edu/plants-temperate-forest

Beeks, J. (2016). *Which of the current diverse ideas on alternative economics are the best for adequately and comprehensively addressing the great transition to climate, energy, and biodiversity sustainability?* (Doctoral dissertation, California Institute of Integral Studies San Francisco, CA). Retrieved from: https://s3.amazonaws.com/academia.edu.documents/45432427/Beeks_Final_5-5.pdf?AWSAccessKeyId=AKIAIWOWYYGZ2Y53UL3A&Expires=1532902143&Signature=ntr3OdGp2YfmMUgBCFOrdsQg4YE%3D&response-content-disposition=inline%3B%20filename

%3DWHICH_OF_THE_CURRENT_DIVERSE_IDEAS
_ON_AL.pdf.

Beeks, J. & Ziko, A. (2018). Internalizing economic externalities on the macroeconomic stage. Exploring and expanding Paul Hawken's *The Ecology of Commerce: A Declaration of Sustainability* for globalized solutions. *European Journal of Sustainable Development Research*, 2(1), 3. doi: 10.20897/ejosdr/76752.

Benyus, J. M. (1997). *Biomimicry*. New York, NY: William Morrow.

Boone, Christopher. (November 21, 2019). Personal Communication.

Borunda, A. (March, 2, 2020). How beef eaters in cities are draining rivers in the American West. *National Geographic*. Retrieved from https://www.nationalgeographic.com/science/2020/03 /burger-water-shortages-colorado-river-western-us/

Carson, R. (1962). *Silent Spring*. New York, NY: Houghton Mifflin Company.

Carrington, D. P. (July 10, 2017). Earth's sixth mass extinction event under way, scientists warn. *The Guardian*. Retrieved from

https://www.theguardian.com/environment/2017/jul/1
0/earths-sixth-mass-extinction-event-already-
underway-scientists-warn

Chesapeake Bay Program. (2020). Plankton. Retrieved
from
https://www.chesapeakebay.net/discover/ecosystem/pl
ankton

CO_2Now.org. (2020). *What the world needs to watch.*
Retrieved from https://www.co2.earth

Davenport, C. & Friedman, L. (2018, July 22).
Lawmakers, lobbyists and the Administration join
forces to overhaul the Endangered Species Act. *New
York Times*, pp. 1.

EPA. (2020). Estuaries and the national estuary
program. U.S. Environmental Protection Agency.
Retrieved from https://www.epa.gov/nep

Faucheux, M. (2017). Plants and animals that live in
rivers and streams. *Sciencing.* Retrieved from https://
sciencing.com/plants-animals-that-live-in-rivers-
streams-13427954.html

FWSR. (2020). Salmon and Steelhead restoration.
Friends of the White Salmon River. Retrieved from
https://friendsofthewhitesalmon.org/issues-2/habitat/

Global Alliance for the Rights of Nature. (2019).
Universal Declaration of Rights of Mother Earth.
Retrieved from https://therightsofnature.org/universal-
declaration/.

Global Exchange. (2017, October). The Stillheart
Declaration.Retrieved from
https://www.movementrights.org/resources/RONStillh
eart.pdf.

Gordon, Gwendolyn J. (2018). "Environmental
Personhood." *Columbia Journal of Environmental
Law*. 43(1), pg. 49-91.

Greenbug Energy (2016). The anatomy of a diversion
hydro site. Retrieved from http://greenbugenergy.com/
get-educated-knowledge/anatomy-diversion-site

Halstead, J. (n.d.). Do trees have rights? Toward an
ecological politics. *Gods and Radical Press*. Retrieved
from https://abeautifulresistance.org/site/2018/01/30/
do-trees-have-rights-toward-an-ecological-politics

Hallmann, C. A., Sorg, M., Jongejans, E., Siepel, H.,
Hofland, N., Schwan, H., ... & Goulson, D. (2017). More
than 75 percent decline over 27 years in total flying
insect biomass in protected areas. *PloS one, 12*(10),
e0185809.

Harris, A. (2018). Ten examples of a natural ecosystem. Retrieved from https://sciencing.com/10-examples-natural-ecosystem-7836.html

Hawken, P. (2010). *The ecology of commerce: A declaration of sustainability* (3rd ed.). New York, NY: Harper Collins Business.

Hawken, P. (2017). *Drawdown: The most comprehensive plan ever proposed to reverse global warming.* New York, NY: Penguin Books.

Houghton, J. T. (1996). *Climate change 1995: The science of climate change: Contribution of working group I to the second assessment report of the intergovernmental panel on climate change.* Cambridge, UK: Cambridge University Press.

Howard, J. (2017, Jan 10). Endangered Species Act facing its own extinction? *American Bird Conservancy.* Retrieved from
    https://abcbirds.org/endangered-species-act-facing-own-extinction/?gclid=CjwKCAjw-dXaBRAEEiwAbwCi5hxR5yvFLzdRvg6yrPNxJbjBajL2Zzb7BSAXzPFz5XqAHapvq85dBoCNKIQAvD_BwE

Ito, M. (May, 2017). Nature's rights: A new paradigm for environmental protection. *Ecologist.* Retrieved from https://theecologist.org/2017/may/09/natures-rights-new-paradigm-environmental-protection

Jackson, T. (2009). Beyond the growth economy. *Journal of Industrial Ecology, 13*(4), 487–490. doi:10.1111/j.1530-9290.2009.00151.x

Kauffman, Craig M. and Martin, Pamela L. (2017). "Can Rights of Nature Make Development. More Sustainable? Why Some Ecuadorian lawsuits Succeed and Others Fail." *World Development.* 92, pg. 30-142.

Kerlin, K. (June, 12, 2020). There's still time to save about half of Earth's land. *Futurity.*

Retrieved from https://www.futurity.org/land-conservation-human-influence-2385082/

Kincaid, Eden. (2019). "'Rights of Nature' in translation: Assemblage geographies, boundary objects, and translocal social movements." *Transaction of the Institute of British Geographers.* 44(3), pg. 555-570.

Klugler, J. (2014). The sixth great extinction is underway – and we're to blame. Time science, July 25, 2014. Retrieved from http://time.com/3035872/sixth-great-extinction/.

Kolbert, E. (2020). Where have all the insects gone. *National Geographic.* May, 2020, 40-65.

Krosby, M., Breckheimer, I., Pierce, D. J., Singleton, P. H., Hall, S. A., Halupka, K. C., ... & Schuett-Hames, J. P. (2015). Focal species and landscape "naturalness" corridor models offer complementary approaches for connectivity conservation planning. *Landscape ecology, 30*(10), 2121-2132.

Leopold, Aldo. (1949). "A Sand County Almanac, And Sketches Here and There" New York: Oxford University Press.

Macy, J., & Johnstone, C. (2012). *Active hope: How to face the mess we're in without going crazy.* San Francisco, CA: New World Library.

Mass, K. (2016). How do we count microbes? University of Connecticut. Retrieved from https://mars.uconn.edu/2016/04/14/how-do-you-count-microbes/

McGregor, Joan. (November 5, 2019). Personal Communication.

Marris, E. (June, 5, 2020). This map shows where on Earth humans aren't. *National Geographic.* Retrieved from https://www.nationalgeographic.com/science/2020/06/where-people-arent/?cmpid=org=ngp::mc=crm-email::src=ngp::cmp=editorial::add=

SpecialEdition_Escape_20200611&rid=FBCD6CCF072
0EA63A946EA4BDAA29693

McCully, P. (n.d.). Dams and water quality.
International Rivers. Retrieved from
https://www.internationalrivers.org/dams-and-water-quality

Meadows, D. H. (2008). Thinking in systems. A primer.
White River Junction: VT: Chelsea Green Publishing

Mickey, S., Kelly, S. & Robbert, A. (2017). The variety of integral ecologies: Nature, culture, and knowledge in the planetary era. Suny Press: New York, NY.

Millennium Ecosystem Assessment. (2005a).
Ecosystems and human well-being: Synthesis.
Washington, DC: Island Press.

Millennium Ecosystem Assessment. (2005b). *Living beyond our means: Natural assets and human well-being: Statement of the MA board.*
Retrieved from   http://www.millenniumassessment.org/en/BoardStatement.html.

Millennium Ecosystem Assessment. (2005c).
Millennium ecosystem assessment: Statement of the MA board. Retrieved from

http://www.millenniumassessment.org/en/Reports.ht
ml

Montuori, A. (2005). Gregory Bateson and the promise
of transdisciplinarity. *Cybernetics and Human
Knowing, 12*(1-2), 147-158.

Montuori, A. (2008). Foreword: Transdisciplinarity. In
B. Nicolescu (Ed.), *Transdisciplinarity: Theory and
practice* (pp. ix–xvii). Cresskill, NJ: Hampton Press.

Nelson, R. (2020). Boreal forests – Taiga. Untamed
Science. Retrieved from
https://untamedscience.com/biology/biomes/taiga/

Nix, S. (2019). Tropical Rainforests and Biodiversity.
Thoughtco. Retrieved from

https://www.thoughtco.com/tropical-rainforests-and-
biodiversity-1341814

NOAA. (2020a). What is the intertidal zone? National
Oceanic and Atmospheric Administration.
Retrieved from
https://oceanservice.noaa.gov/facts/intertidal-
zone.html

NOAA. (2020b). Coral reef ecosystems. National
Oceanic and Atmospheric Administration.
Retrieved from

https://www.noaa.gov/education/resource-collections/
marine-life/coral-reef-ecosystems

Noss, R.F., LaRoe, E.T., Scott, J.M. (n.a.). Endangered Ecosystems of the United States: A Preliminary Assessment of Loss and Degradation. Retrieved from https://www.fwspubs.org/doi/suppl/10.3996/022015-JFWM-008/suppl_file/022015-jfwm-008.s5.pdf.

Nunez, C. (2019). Tundras, explained. *National Geographic*. Retrieved from https://www.nationalgeographic.com/environment/habitats/tundra-biome/

Oceana. (2020). Open ocean. Oceana: Protecting the world's oceans. Retrieved from https://oceana.org/marine-life/marine-science-and-ecosystems/open-ocean

Oppenlander, R. (2013). *Food choice and sustainability: Why buying local, eating less meat, and taking baby steps won't work*. Minneapolis, MN: Langdon Street Press.

Pearce, F. (2006). *When the rivers run dry*. Boston, MA: Beacon Press. ISBN -13: 978-0-8070-8573-8

Poehler, B. (Aug. 10, 2018). Detroit dam fish passage project has cost $8 million so far: To cost $100 million or more. *Statesman Journal*. Retrieved from https://www.statesmanjournal.com/story/news/local/stayton/2018/08/10/detroit-dam-fish-passage-project-cost/940704002/

Predator Conservation Alliance. (2001). Restoring the prairie dog ecosystem of the Great Plains. Learning from the past to ensure the prairie dog's future. Retrieved from http://omnilearn.net/esacourse/pdfs/prairiedogreport2001.pdf

Pye, Oliver. (2019). "Commodifying sustainability: Development, nature and politics in the palm oil industry." *World Development*. 121, pg. 218-228.

Rogers, P. C., & McAvoy, D. J. (2018). Mule deer impede Pando's recovery: Implications for
        aspen resilience from a single-genotype forest. *PLOS One*. Retrieved from
        https://journals.plos.org/plosone/article?id=10.1371/journal.pone.0203619

Schlosberg, D. (2001). Three Dimensions of Environmental and Ecological Justice. 1-25. Retrieved 2020, from https://ecpr.eu/Filestore/PaperProposal/5ef89598-7149-4b8d-82b3-567750b392f6.pdf

Senge, P. (2006). *The fifth discipline: The art and practice of the learning organization.* New York, NY: Doubleday Publishing.

Singer, Peter. (1989). "All Animals Are Equal" in *Animal Rights and Human Obligations.* New Jersey: Prentice-Hall.

Slideplayer.com (n.d.) Nature as property and the Land Ethic. [Image]. Retrieved from

https://www.google.com/url?sa=i&url=https%3A%2F%2Fheqaquqixurezifyg.holidaysanantonio.com%2Fland-ethic8485kh.html&psig=AOvVaw2oZrNSq4H5L_cDBN FORDQj &ust =1592071214256000&source=images&cd=vfe&ved=0C AIQjRxqFwo TCKCsosvt_OkCFQAAAAAdAAAAABA6

Solomon, S. (2007). *Climate change 2007—The physical science basis: Working group I contribution to the fourth assessment report of the IPCC.* Cambridge, MA: Cambridge University Press.

Steffen, W., Broadgate, W., Deutsch, L., Gaffney, O., & Ludwig, C. (2015). The trajectory of the anthropocene: The great acceleration. *The Anthropocene Review, 2*(1), 81–98.

Stone, C. D. (1972). Should Trees Have Standing-- Toward Legal Rights for Natural Objects. *S. Cal. l. rev., 45,* 450

Tamaqua Borough Sewage Sludge Ordinance. (2006). Tamaqua Borough, Schuylkill County, Pennsylvania Ordinance No. 612 of 2006. Retrieved from http://files.harmonywithnatureun.org/uploads/upload 666.pdf.

Taus, J. (Mar., 2016). Shoot. Shove. Shut Up. *International Society for Endangered Cats, (ISEC) Canada.* Retrieved from https://wildcatconservation.org/shoot-shovel-shut-2/

Taylor, P. W. (1981). The ethics of respect for nature. *Environmental ethics, 3*(3), 197-218.

Taylor, Paul W. (1981). 'The Ethics of Respect for Nature." Brooklyn, NY: Brooklyn College of the City University of New York.

Tripati, A. K., Roberts, C. D., & Eagle, R. A. (2009). Coupling of CO2 and ice sheet stability over major climate transitions of the last 20 million years. *Science, 326*(5958), 1394–1397. doi:10.1126/science.1178296

UCMP (2020a). The grassland biome. *UC Museum of Paleontology.* Retrieved From https://ucmp.berkeley.edu/exhibits/biomes/grasslands.php

UCMP. (2020b). The desert biome. *UC Museum of Paleontology.* Retrieved from https://ucmp.berkeley.edu/exhibits/biomes/deserts.php

United Nations Division for Sustainable Development. (1992, June). United Nations Conference on Environment & Development Rio de Janeiro, Brazil 3 to 14 June 1992. Retrieved from https://sustainabledevelopment.un.org/content/documents/Agenda21.pdf.

USACE (2012). Columbia River Fish Mitigation. U.S. Army Corps of Engineers. Retrieved from https://www.nwd.usace.army.mil/Media/Fact-Sheets/Fact-Sheet-Article-View/Article/475821/columbia-river-fish-mitigation/

USFWS. (2020). Marbled Murrelet. Retrieved from https://www.fws.gov/oregonfwo/articles.cfm?id=149489445

Vogel, G. (May 10, 2017). Where have all the insects
gone? *Science*. Retrieved from
https://www.sciencemag.org/news/2017/05/where-
have-all-insects-gone

Waldman, J. (April4, 2013). Blocked migration: Fish
ladders on U.S. dams are not effective. *Yale
Environment 360*. Published at the Yale School of
Forestry & Environmental Studies

Warne, K. (2019). "The Whanganui River in New
Zealand is a legal person. A nearby forest is too. Soon,
the government will grant a mountain legal personhood
as well. Here's how it happened, and what it may mean."
National Geographic. Retrieved from
https://www.nationalgeographic.com/culture/2019/04
/maori-river-in-new-zealand-is-a-legal-person/

Wells, J. (2013). *Complexity and sustainability*. New
York, NY: Routledge. White, Rob. (2014). "Indigenous
communities, environmental protection and restorative
justice. (New South Wales, Australia, New Zealand)."
Australian Indigenous Law Review. 18(2), pg. 43-54.

Winton, R. S., Calamita, E. & Wehrli, B. (2019). Reviews
and synthesis: Dams, water quality and tropical
reservoir stratification. *Biogeosciences (16)*, 1657-1671.
https://doi.org/10.5194/bg-16-1657-2019

Yale, (2020). Boreal forest ecology. Global Forest Atlas. Retrieved from https://globalforestatlas.yale.edu/boreal-forest/boreal-ecoregions-ecology/boreal-forest-ecology

Zartner, D. (2019, September 16). Giving legal rights to nature could reduce public threats like toxic algae. *Popular Science*. Retrieved from https://www.popsci.com/giving-legal-rights-to-nature/

Publications of the Green Economics Institute ©

The Green Economics Institute Publishing House has now published over 100 titles from leading authors and innovative thinkers with new ideas and change making solutions for today's pressing issues. Our books are created in Open Office and many have around 30 different writers and voices in each book, so that a variety of novel perspectives can be introduced from all around the world.

Economics Books

Handbook of Green Economics: A Practitioner's Guide (2012) Edited By Miriam Kennet, Eleni Courea, Alan Bouquet and Ieva Pepinyte ISBN 9781907543036

Green Economics Methodology: An Introduction (2012) Edited By Tone Berg (Norway), Aase Seeberg (Norway) and Miriam Kennet ISBN 978190754357

The Green Economics Reader (2012) Edited By Miriam Kennet ISBN 9781907543265

Rebalancing the Economy (2014) Edited by Christopher Brook, Cambridge University and Miriam Kennet. ISBN9781907543845

Economics of Social Justice (2015) Edited by Miriam Kennet, Iolanda Cum and Sabeeta Nathan ISBN 9781907543463

Growth for Sustainability – A Critique of Economics for the Post Oil Age (2016) Edited by Keissi Prendushi (Italy and Albania), Miriam Kennet (UK) and Federica Oriana Savarino (Sicily, Italy) ISBN 9781907543135

The Future of Income, Labour and Work (2017) Edited by Miriam Kennet. ISBN 9781907543531

Finance Books

The Greening of Global Finance: Reforming Global Finance c (2013) Edited By Professor Graciela Chichilnisky (USA and Argentina), Michelle S. Gale de Oliveira (USA and Brazil), Miriam Kennet, Professor Maria Madi (Brazil) and Professor Chow Fah Yee (Malaysia) ISBN 9781907543401

The Reform of Global Banking (2015) Professor Maria Madi and Kamile Buskavait. ISBN 9781907543203

Values, Valuation and Valuing (2017) Edited by Miriam Kennet (UK), Pamela Harling (UK), Maria Madi (Brazil and Argentina), Karen Windham Lord (Brazil and UK) ISBN 9781907543555

Geographies of Green Economics

Greening the Global Economy (2013) Edited by Sofia Amaral (Portugal) and Miriam Kennet ISBN 9781907543944

Green Economics: The Greening of Asia and China (2012) Edited by Miriam Kennet (UK) and

Norfayanti Kamaruddin (Malaysia) ISBN 9781907543234

Green Economics: Voices of Africa (2012) Edited By Miriam Kennet, Amana Winchester, Mahelet Mekonnen and Chidi Magnus Onuoha ISBN 9781907543098

The Greening of Eastern Europe (2013) Edited By Miriam Kennet and Dr Sandra Gusta (Latvia) ISBN 9781907543418

Green Economics: The Greening of Indonesia (2013) Edited By Dr Dessy Irwati and Dr Stephan Onggo (Indonesia) ISBN 9781907543821

The Greening of Latin America (2013) Edited By Michelle S. Gale de Oliveira (USA and Brazil), Maria Fernanda Caporale Madi (Brazil), Carlos Francisco Restituyo Vassallo (Dominican Republic) and Miriam Kennet ISBN 9781907543876

Africa: Transition to a Green Economy (2013) Edited By Dr Chidi Magnus (Nigeria) ISBN 9781907543364

Green Economics & India (2014) Edited by Professor Natalie West, Professor Indira Dutta, Odeta Grabauskaitė, Kanupriya Bhagat and Miriam Kennet ISBN 9781907543500

The Greening of the Mediterranean Economy (2013) Edited by Miriam Kennet, Dr Michael Briguglio, Dr Enrico Tezza, Michelle S Gale de Oliveira and Doaa Salman ISBN 9781907543906

The European Economy: Crisis and Recovery (2014) Edited by Miriam Kennet ISBN 9781907543463

The Eastern European Economy, Policy and Practise for Recovery (2014) Professor Dr Dzintra Astaja (Latvia) and Odeta Grabauskaitė (Lithuania) ISBN 9781907543890

The Greening of Italy: Crisis and Recovery (2014) Edited by Alberto Truccolo ISBN 9781097543920

Health and Well Being Books

The Greening of Health and Well Being (2012) Edited by Katherine Kennet, Michelle Gale de Oliveira and Miriam Kennet ISBN 9781907543760

NHS Continuing Health Care (2016) Edited by Peter Lang (UK) ISBN 9781907543753

Social Policy Books

The Vintage Generation, the Rocking Chair Revolution (2015) Edited by Miriam Kennet and Birgit Meinhard – Schiebel (Austria) ISBN 9781907543517

Citizen's Income and Green Economics (2012) By Clive Lord, edited by Judith Felton and Miriam Kennet ISBN 9781907543074

Green Economics: Women's Unequal Pay and Poverty (2012) Edited By Miriam Kennet, Michelle S Gale de Oliveira, Judith Felton and Amana Winchester ISBN 9781907543081

Young People: Green Jobs, Employment and Education (2012) Edited By Miriam Kennet and Juliane Goeke (Germany) ISBN 9781907543258

The Philosophy of Social Justice (2015) Edited by Miriam Kennet and Samuel Gilmore ISBN 9781907543739

Fairtrade (2016) Jessica Bosseaux ISBN 9781907543708

Energy and Climate Policy

Green Economics and Climate Change (2012) Edited By Miriam Kennet and Winston Ka-Ming Mak (Hong Kong and UK)

Green Economics: The Greening of Energy Policies (2012) Edited By Ryota Koike and Miriam Kennet ISBN 9781907543326

Rolling Back the Tide of Climate Change: Energy Policy in the USA and China (2015) Professor Peter Yang Autumn 2015 ISBN 9781907543777

Renewables are Getting Cheaper (2016) Edited by Professor Peter Yang ISBN 9781907543722

Biomassa Algale (2015) Iolanda Cum. ISBN 9781907543982

Renewable Energy Economics in Egypt and the MENA Region (2016) by Hend Ahmed Mohamed Mohamed Saadeldin Edited by Francesca Galli (2016) ISBN 9781907543173

Renewable Energy Choices: Stories from the Transition to Renewables (2016) Jasmeet Phagoora, Federica Savarino,(Italy) Miriam Kennet and Iolanda Cum (Italy) ISBN 9781907543166

Food, Farming and Agriculture

Green Economics & Food, Farming and Agriculture (2013) Edited by Michelle S. Gale de Oliveira, Rose Blackett-Ord and Miriam Kennet ISBN 9781907543449

Greening the Food on Your Plate (2013) Edited by Michelle S. Gale de Oliveira, Rose Blackett-Ord and Miriam Kennet ISBN 9781907543654

Biodiversity, conservation and animal protection Books

Biodiversity Loss: The Variety of Life Under Threat (2015) Anna Wainer, Odeta Grabauskaitė and Miriam Kennet ISBN 9781907543227

Lifestyle Books

The Green Transport Revolution (2013) Edited By Richard Holcroft and Miriam Kennet ISBN 9781907543968

Green Poetry, Art and Photography (2013) Edited by Dr Matt Rinaldi, Rose Blackett-Ord, Friedericke Oeser Prasse and Miriam Kennet ISBN 9781907543784

The Green Built Environment: A Handbook (2012) Edited By Miriam Kennet and Judith Felton ISBN 9781907543067

Building Sustainable Communities: Life and Thoughts of Henry Cox (2016) Edited by Henry Fieglar ISBN 9781907543197

Philosophy Books

Integrating Ethics, Social Responsibility and Governance (2013) Edited by Tore Audin Hedin, Michelle Gale de Oliveira, Miriam Kennet ISBN 9781907543395

The Philosophical Basis of the Green Movement (2013) Edited by Professor Michael Benfield, Miriam Kennet and Michelle Gale de Oliveira (Brazil) ISBN 9781907543548

Green Culture, Cultures and Philosophy (2016) Edited by Nelly Eysholdt and Miriam Kennet ISBN9781907543661

Migration Books

Introducing Migration (2016) Edited by Henry Fieglar and Miriam Kennet ISBN 9781907543210

Printed by Printforce, United Kingdom